Rock, Rhythm and Reels

REF 780.92 ROC C.1
Rock, rhythm and reels :
Canada's East Coast
musicians on stage /

Canada's East Coast Musicians on Stage

Rock, Rhythm and Reels

REF 780.92 ROC C.1
Rock, rhythm and reels :
Canada's East Coast
musicians on stage /

Edited by Lee Fleming

RAGWEED
THE ISLAND PUBLISHER

Copyright © Lee Fleming, 1997

Individual copyright to their articles is retained by the contributors.

All rights reserved. No part of this book may be reproduced or transmitted in any form or by any means whatsoever without permission of the publisher, except by a reviewer, who may quote brief passages in a review.

Edited by: Jennifer Glossop

Cover photographs: Barra MacNeil's photo by Denise Grant; Four the Moment's photo by Photo 67 (Kuch); Ashley MacIsaac's photo by Derek Shapton; Anne Murray's photo by James O'Mara; Sarah McLachlan's photo by Dennis Keeley; and Sloan's photo by Catherine Stockhausen.

Printed and bound in Canada by: D.W. Friesen

Ragweed Press acknowledges the generous support of the Canada Council.

Lyrics to "Please Don't Sell Nova Scotia" used with the kind permission of Tessa Productions.

Published by:
Ragweed Press
P.O. Box 2023
Charlottetown, PEI
Canada C1A 7N7

REF
780.92
ROC
C.1

Canadian Cataloguing in Publication Data

Main enty under title:

    Rock, rhythm and reels.

    ISBN 0-921556-65-9

1. Musicians — Atlantic Provinces. 2. Music trade — Atlantic Provinces. I. Fleming, Lee, 1957-

ML3563.R682 1997   780'.92'2715   C96-950242-7

Acknowledgements

I wish to thank Ragweed Press, publisher of great books from and about this region. In particular, thanks *mille fois* to Sibyl Frei, managing editor, whose amazing organizational prowess and attention to detail kept this project moving always forward. Janet Riopelle is responsible for the beautiful design that makes this book such a joy to hold, read and browse. Donna Lynn Wigmore and Tammy Pigott did the transcriptions of interviews, a thankless but necessary job, and Donna provided other excellent editorial assistance.

I'd also like to thank Eric MacEwen; Glenn Meisner; Sam Sniderman; Marc Chouinard, Moncton ECMA Co-ordinator; Barbara Nymark, Executive Producer at CBC in Charlottetown, PEI; Jim Hornby; and Jill Richardson, Tourism PEI. Special thanks to Jennifer Glossop, who put her fine editorial touches to each contribution.

In putting together this book, I had a lot of contact with the managers and promoters who work so tirelessly on behalf of their artists. Their work often goes unnoticed and unrecognized by the listening public, but they deserve much credit for their hard work in bringing artists to the public sphere.

Finally, my biggest thanks are offered to the artists who made this book project so rewarding. Their willingness to share their stories, and their exemplary professionalism have made a lasting impression on me, and have given me inspiration in continuing my own journey as a musician.

And they came out of the East Coast to capture Canada, and then the World, with their songs and music.

God made them artists, but you have made them stars.

These are the stories of how some of those that live beside you, with the means of modern technology, now roam the globe, in spirit and in body.

I am proud to have been part of their growth.

— Sam, the Record Man, Sniderman, C.M.

Preface

The month of February on Prince Edward Island is usually endured — huge snowstorms, sub-zero temperatures, and few jobs to tide us over until summer — and then quickly forgotten. This all changed in 1996. The East Coast Music Association's annual music extravaganza took place in PEI and shook out the February blues. We were treated to a five-day feast of plentiful and varied musical genres, styles and acts. Everyone touched by the ECMAs — musicians, songwriters, producers and promoters, the fans and volunteers at all the venues, as well as the television viewers of the gala awards show — took pleasure in the amazing phenomenon of Canada's East Coast music.

Wanting to capture the excitement and the diversity of East Coast music for book lovers, I approached Ragweed Press about doing a book that would celebrate the East Coast music phenomenon. In June 1996, with their enthusiastic go ahead, I embarked upon an unforgettable five-month musical adventure.

There are many talented musicians from this region; working from a list of over 100 musicians, my challenge was to select forty-seven artists to represent the vibrancy and diversity of the music here. It was important to find a balance between well-established and up-and-coming musicians, to represent each part of our region, and to show the variety of styles and cultures that make up East Coast music. The musicians profiled in *Rock, Rhythm and Reels* are a wonderful combination that truly represent what is so exciting about East Coast music.

Since summer is a very busy time for musicians, I decided to interview each contributor or group, rather than expect them to write something for me. With tape recorder in hand, I met with artists before their performances, at their homes or hotel rooms, on my back verandah and over the phone. I enquired about each musician's or band's background, how they came to be professional

"We were treated to a five-day musical feast."

> "The Maritimes is clearly a part of them and they are a part of the Maritimes."

musicians, and what their take was on the seemingly sudden success of East Coast musicians. I was also interested in any advice they had for people considering a career in music. To add levity, I asked the contributors for funny or unusual anecdotes from their careers. (In the editing of each contribution, I removed my voice so that each story could flow uninterrupted.) I was treated to engaging repartee, strongly held opinion, and trademark East Coast humour. And I caught some excellent performances into the bargain!

The easy and relaxed conversations I had with which some of the bigger stars, and their interest in this project, were reminders of the strong ties to culture and community that make up part of the East Coast music phenomenon. It was a great pleasure to receive the steady stream of CDs and demo tapes that were sent along, and even more of a pleasure to listen to the music as I worked at the editing of the contributions. And I certainly found myself in some funny situations, like the evening phone call with Darrell Bernard, from Sons of Membertou. After a long chat, I got off the phone only to find that I hadn't recorded a word of our conversation! I called him back and explained, and he very graciously did the whole interview again. Or my interview with Teresa Doyle that ended in her extensive gardens, picking quite a few choice PEI raspberries.

The forty-seven contributors are a varied lot: solo artists, family groups, a choir; the well-established and up-and-coming; those locally based and those who spend most of their time touring. They come from many corners of this region, including one group from the Magdalen Islands in the Gulf of St. Lawrence. There are also musicians who were born here but left early in their careers for other parts of Canada. Even if they haven't lived here for many years, the Maritimes is clearly a part of them and they are a part of the Maritimes. Other musicians who "came from away" now consider the East Coast their permanent home. The majority of musicians, however, were born and raised here and have never left except for sojourns into the larger world.

The musical styles represented in this book illustrate just how diverse East Coast music is and always has been. People from outside the region often perceive East Coast music as being Celtic or

Gaelic — a not unreasonable assumption given the number of those players who are finally getting the recognition they deserve. However, the East Coast's cultural history is rich, and this book is a reflection of that diversity, with contributors who are Mi'kmaq, Acadian, Afro-Canadian, and of Scottish, Irish, English and Dutch-German origin. Musical styles are just as varied: blues, jazz, pop, gospel, alternative, country, folk, rock, bluegrass, classical, and children's, to name only some.

Many East Coast artists prefer not to label their music. They are striving to transcend any one musical genre and to create something new. Nonetheless, all acknowledge that the musical traditions they grew up with — whether heard in their kitchens, in their churches, on their radios or on stage — have found a way into their music.

It is the variety and energy of their music that has created the East Coast music phenomenon — a phenomenon rooted in the land, culture, tradition and history of this region. Very much like the story-based East Coast culture itself, the forty-seven profiles in *Rock, Rhythm and Reels* enlighten us about this musical wave. Through hearing the voices of people who make up the music scene here, we understand more about this exciting, growing phenomenon.

This book chronicles a specific time and specific players in this region's musical development. It captures the thoughts and stories of some of the most important musicians at work right now. For reasons of space and time limitations, there are notables absent from this collection, and many who have gone before, laying the groundwork for the success that many East Coast musicians are currently enjoying. And there are other artists, poised to enter the spotlight. JP Cormier put it aptly: The musicians that are now being noticed by the rest of the world are "just the tip of the iceberg."

As we approach the new millennium, the time has never been better nor the prospects brighter for Atlantic Canadian musicians. Still, I was reminded time and again that the first and best impetus for success is the love of the music. Veteran jazz saxophonist Bucky Adams summed it up: "If the money comes, great. But if it doesn't come, thank the Lord you had the chance to please some

> "Atlantic Canadians have always known how to laugh, sing and play through good times and hard times."

people on the way through." Atlantic Canadians have always known how to laugh, sing and play through good times and hard times. Perhaps that is why there are so many amazing musicians from this end of the country.

The book you are holding in your hands is the result of my fascinating exploration of music from Canada's East Coast. *Rock, Rhythm and Reels* is everything and more than I could have hoped for: an informative, beautifully designed book full of personal stories, that will find its place in collectors' hands for years to come.

Lee Fleming
November 1996

Contents

Introduction (by Eric MacEwen) 15
Charles "Bucky" Adams 20
Debbie Adshade 24
Barachois 28
Barra MacNeils 32
John Allen Cameron 36
Holly Cole 40
Stompin' Tom Connors 44
J.P. Cormier 48
Lee Cremo 52
Damhnait Doyle 56
Teresa Doyle 60
Eagle Feather 64
Four the Moment 68
Annick Gagnon 72
Lennie Gallant 76
Goodspeed/Staples 80
Gospel Heirs 84
Great Big Sea 88
Bruce Guthro 92
Ron Hynes 96
jale 100

Roy Johnstone	104
Mary Jane Lamond	108
Ray Legere	112
Ashley MacIsaac	116
Dave MacIsaac	120
Natalie MacMaster	124
Scott Macmillan	128
Rita MacNeil	132
Theresa Malenfant	136
Doris Mason	140
Dutch Mason	144
Sarah McLachlan	148
Matt Minglewood	152
Modabo	156
Anne Murray	160
Nova Scotia Mass Choir	164
Scott Parsons	168
The Rankin Family	172
Rawlins Cross	176
sandbox	180
Sloan	184
Laura Smith	188
Sons of Membertou	192
Kim Stockwood	196
Suroît	200
Duncan Wells	204

Introduction

Music has always been a mainstay of life on Canada's East Coast. For the Aboriginal peoples of this region, music was an integral part of daily life and an important part of spiritual celebrations. The drumming circle was the heartbeat of communal life, and chants were passed down from generation to generation.

Music came from everywhere. Settlers brought indigenous music and dance to their new home. The Scotts and Irish brought fiddle tunes. Frequent community dances called for tunes that young and old could enjoy, so local musicians played strathspeys, marches, jigs and reels. Acadians contributed their own folk songs, fiddle music and dances, including the Acadian Quadrille. The English brought ballads, sea shanties and church music. The Black community had rich gospel and folk music traditions as well.

It was a largely rural society, and livelihoods were tied to the sea and the land. In the days before radios and TV, people would gather in each other's homes to trade stories, sing songs and stepdance to the joyful sound of the fiddle, the squeeze box or the pump organ. One can imagine walking through a village on a clear, crisp winter night, seeing the plume of wood smoke against the night sky and the warm glow of the kerosene-lit homes. A tune carried gently on the wind would say, "Welcome, friend. There's always room for one more."

Atlantic Canadians come from a strong romantic tradition, where family, friends and neighbours were all cared for and where our creative expression was found through music and dance. Geographic isolation served only to strengthen the richness and diversity of music and dance. During poor economic times, music was an antidote to the difficulties of daily existence.

The advent of radio introduced us to music other than our own. Fortunately, we had our own radio shows, and some of our musicians became quite famous. During the 1930s and 1940s, radio

> "A tune carried gently on the wind would say, 'Welcome, friend. There's always room for one more'."

> "The strong sense of storytelling evident in our lyrics and the timeless melodies of our music speak to a universal audience."

stations featured live music shows. Suddenly Don Messer and the Islanders, Winston Scotty Fitzgerald, Hank Snow and Wilf Carter, among others, became household names.

Gradually, however, more and more of the music played on radio came from the commercial centres of North America. The recording studios, management, promotion and distribution were all located elsewhere, and our music no longer had an opportunity to grow to its full potential. Despite this, the tradition of making our own music was alive and well, albeit on a much smaller scale. We still had national successes during this time, but making it in the music business meant leaving home.

In the 1960s, major talents emerged. Anne Murray and Stompin' Tom Connors achieved phenomenal success. And Gene MacLellan was writing songs the world loved. The mid- to late-1970s saw the technology of recording, previously available only in the commercial centres, become more and more affordable and accessible. Gradually recording studios started opening on the East Coast. Just as important, our stable of songwriters and singers was never better. Ron Hynes, Rita MacNeil, Edith Butler, Leon Dubinsky, Jimmy Rankin and Lennie Gallant, to name a few, were all poised for the evolution taking place. It was only a matter of time before North American music made way for the wave of East Coast music.

The annual industry music award show, the East Coast Music Awards, started out in 1988 as a small and unpretentious event to celebrate and nurture our growing music industry. Today the annual ECMA Conference and Trade Show is the single biggest cultural event of the year on the East Coast. It has helped immeasurably to focus attention on the music and to support the incredible momentum happening in the music business here. Through the ECMAs we witness the new talent in the ranks and potential for the future. For many, the awards have been the springboard that has launched them into the broader Canadian and international arena.

Music is a natural part of the culture of the East Coast. The most remarkable quality of our music is that it is at the heart of our East Coast culture. The strong sense of storytelling evident in our lyrics and the timeless melodies of our music speak to a universal audience. And now, for the first time, a book chronicles some of the living history of this phenomenon. *Rock, Rhythm and Reels* is a wonderful look at musicians who exemplify the best of East Coast music. Many were there before "the wave" hit and are proof that a successful music career can span decades. Others demonstrate the many new directions that this wave is headed.

After reading this book, I'm sure you will have a greatly enhanced appreciation of the exciting East Coast music scene. Read on and enjoy.

Eric MacEwen
November 1996

Rock, Rhythm and Reels

Charles "Bucky" Adams

Bucky Adams needs no introduction in the Maritimes' music community. He is Halifax's own legendary saxophone artist and comes from one of Nova Scotia's oldest musical families. His career spans six decades and includes performances with such greats as Louis Armstrong, Dizzy Gillespie, Lionel Hampton, B.B. King and Oscar Peterson. Bucky plays the blues, easy listening and swing — with his own original touch.

"Bucky has a fine musical instinct, a natural feel for the phrase ... his expressive playing rivets attention and opens up a river of communication."

— *The Chronicle-Herald*, Halifax

Ambassador of Jazz

My mother was a Parker. They were part of the Mi'kmaq tribe from down in the Annapolis Valley. My father's side was African. Put that together, and that's what I am.

I come from a big musical family. We've played here ever since Nova Scotia has been here. My mother's family was in the food catering business. My father's family was into vaudeville. In the First World War, my father's uncle had an eighty-piece marching band. Back then there were many Adams musicians. My sons, Anthony and Corey, and I keep on with the tradition. Even Corey's two-year-old son is learning to play the saxophone!

It was always music, just music. My mother put the music into me before I was born. Even in kindergarten and grade one, I was tapping out rhythms on the desk with pencils. My father helped me a lot and tried to teach me to read music. He could read and write any music and play every instrument — not just the keyboards, all the instruments, and there were eighty in his uncle's band! And he had to know how to fix them. He didn't want me to learn music the way he did. His father and uncle beat him across his knuckles and made him learn. He didn't want that for me. He said, "You've got to want to do it. You'll pursue it if you want it."

I started playing trumpet in 1946 and got my first paying job in 1948, when the Barnum and Bailey Circus came to town. They wanted me to travel with them, but I was too young and didn't want to leave home. We never had a school band, but I was with the sea cadets for a few years, blowing bugle. I played for Queen Elizabeth, as a matter of fact, when she made her first trip here in 1953. I picked up the sax the next year. Back then I listened to big-band stuff. The smallest band would have been Louis Armstrong's, which was about six or seven pieces at that time. A lot of those bands made their way to Halifax. I played with Lionel Hampton's band here back in the 1950s.

opening notes

Date of birth
April 25, 1937

Place of birth
Halifax, Nova Scotia

Heritage
Afro-Canadian, Mi'kmaq

Language
English

Current residence
Halifax, Nova Scotia

Instruments
Saxophone, trumpet, bugle

> "Music is a great healer."

In my twenties I married a very nice lady. We've been married forty years and have five children and eleven grandchildren, with a twelfth due to arrive soon. My wife has so much faith in me. That's what's kept me going. I've played with everybody that's anybody, but strictly by ear. I've been blessed with a good ear. I would call myself a jazz musician first and foremost. I play what they call "Liquid Jazz." I've toured just about all of Canada, and down through the States. But I never thought about leaving. I've always loved it here. I have a good feeling here. We're different in a lot of ways. We're easygoing, something you don't get in those big cities where everybody is in too much of a rush even to give you directions. Our music is a little more forgiving. Maybe our music is freer because of the laid-back attitude of the Maritimes. Maybe that's it.

I think the new interest in music from the East Coast will be a good thing. A lot of the talent here is financially strapped. And the whole Black musical community, especially instrumental musicians, is hardly heard from, despite the fact that there has always been a jazz-and-blues scene in this area. There is a legacy of jazz in Nova Scotia. Back in the 1950s we had a great jazz club called the Gerrish Street Hall, a Black dance hall. A lot of the big bands that were booked into the Halifax Forum would go there afterwards.

There are many unsung heroes from the Black community — me included! A lot of the young guys who are playing here today started with me. David James, who, I believe, is one of Canada's finest young drummers, started with me about twenty years ago at the Middle Deck, here in Halifax. In 1985-86 I studied for a year at the music department at St. Francis Xavier. Many of the young people I met there are now very successful musicians. I can see jazz being carried on through those people.

discography

- **Bucky Adams & Basin Street**/Music Stop, 1975
- **Roots: The Current Generation** (2-track, compilation CD)/Jongleur, 1996
- **In A Loving Way**/1997 release

My inspiration stems from the spirit inside. I find music is a great healer. I play with a volunteer senior citizens' band on Wednesday and Friday nights. One of the piano players is eighty-three. The violin player is seventy-nine. These people get so inspired when we start playing. All the music is from the old days, but with a nice little lift to it. The music takes them back. It's like therapy. They forget their aches and pains. They even forget how old they are. You give them so little and they give back so much. I would like to have the band recorded so that people can say, "Hey, you don't have to stop because you are a certain age." That's my inspiration.

You have to live music. You can't learn to play an instrument or take part in the industry one day and quit the next. You have to live it and do it and love it. You don't go into it to get rich, because it's not about the money. If the money comes, great. But if it doesn't come, thank the Lord you had the chance to please some people on the way through. That's about the way I sum it up.

FANfare

Management
Betty Symons,
34 Franklyn Drive,
Beaverbank, NS,
B4G 1A4;
(902) 865-4875 (phone)

Just Getting Better

I was on a national TV show, and just before the countdown was finished, a pad fell off my horn, which means the whole horn won't work. I had to think right fast, so I started to sing. It worked, and I got through the show. But later I got a phone call from a lady in Toronto who said, "Your saxophone playing is fine, but your singing leaves something to be desired." That was twenty-five years ago. I've recently started singing again. I'll have to track that lady down and send her a copy of my new CD. I think she'll like my singing this time around.

Debbie Adshade

"Powerful" is the only word to describe Debbie Adshade in performance. Singing with a dramatic intensity that brings lyrics and music to life, she paints pictures and tells stories that evoke the divine in all of us. She communicates emotions, joining listener with performer in a powerful musical experience.

As a professional performer since her teen years, Debbie has sung in concert with many exceptional musicians.

"Adshade's lead vocals are stylized and engrossing. She has a powerful expressive voice ... She exploits falsetto and doesn't hesitate to swoop several octaves in a single line."
— *Daily News*, Halifax

The Infinity of Music

I was in grade nine when I discovered my voice — performing live into a hairbrush in my room. I think it was a Dionne Warwick version of a Righteous Brothers song. I soon took my show on the road — or, more accurately, to the schoolyard — where I received no bumps or bruises for my efforts. Encouraged by this, I began playing guitar. After mastering two chords, I wrote my first twenty-five songs. I went on to perform at noon hours in the third-floor girls' lavatory at Saint John High School. The acoustics there were great!

In grade eleven, amid a delicious mix of terror and ecstasy, I performed with my girl friend, Harriet Murray, at the school's variety show. We did our own Gregorian-chant version of a Black Sabbath ballad and Melanie's "Lay Down." Harriet played guitar for that song because I hadn't quite figured out the F-chord yet.

The same year I received an invitation to perform with a high-school rock band. Our first stage performance was especially memorable for the thundering sound of the bass amp being knocked over by the opening curtain.

Inspiration came easily with the fertile music of the late 1960s and early 1970s — Jimi Hendrix; Janis Joplin; Joni Mitchell; Crosby, Stills, Nash and Young; and Grace Slick. I enjoyed wrapping my voice around their sounds and stealing licks from these great artists.

At present, I am attempting to lose my influences and develop my own sound. Over the past two years, I have been inspired by my producer and bass player, Lloyd Hanson. His belief in steering clear of the well-travelled musical pathways and going for fresh ground has helped me push ahead and try for a more distinct tone. I feel each performance is an opportunity to unite forces with an audience. With energy flowing back and forth, it can be very spiritual. It is therefore important to convey a positive and uplifting message — both in a sonic and a lyrical sense. The songs on my

opening notes

Date of birth
November 20, 1955; Scorpio

Place of birth
Saint John, New Brunswick

Heritage
½ French, ¼ Scottish, ⅛ Welsh, 1/32 Native, remainder unknown

Languages
English and some really bad French

Current residence
Saint John, New Brunswick

Instruments
Vocals, guitar, piano, rainstick

> "You must learn to express your own spirit."

second CD, *Alchemy*, are inspired by different philosophical and religious views, both ancient and modern. I've long been fascinated by the variety of life paths and wisdom traditions we embrace to nurture our human spirit.

Here on the East Coast we are perhaps less removed from a community spirit than more cosmopolitan centres are. We must rekindle that sense of community. As individuals, we must support our local businesses and cottage industries. We need to look out for one another and respect the land. The music-maker's situation is similar. The independent music movement has become a force. We need to continue in that vein. We must persuade folks to avoid the disposable music and images that are being bottled and packaged by the large companies. The music made in the kitchens of the East Coast is a gift to us all. We need to keep it real!

When I think of East Coast music, the images that come to mind are fiddles and Celtic sounds with a rich, warm, down-home flavour. Recently, innovative players like Ashley MacIsaac and Great Big Sea have been giving this music a fresh kick. The world's cultural and musical boundaries are increasingly merging and flowing to create a new and unified world sound. I like to think that music will evolve until there are no boundaries.

When I was younger, I moved around a bit. The people I met elsewhere, especially in the rural areas, often reminded me of the folks at home. I think wherever you find a close community you will find caring people. However, when you are born with an ocean at your front door, you are never entirely comfortable anywhere else. I remember living out west in the 1970s. After some time, I began experiencing an overwhelming sense of suffocation. It wasn't until I came home and dangled my toes in the ocean that I realized what a powerful influence the East Coast and the Atlantic Ocean held on me.

discography

- **The Thunder God's Wife**/independent, 1995
- **Alchemy**/independent, 1997 release

My advice to young musicians is to listen to your own drummer. Enjoy your influences and learn from them. Ultimately, though, you must learn to express your own spirit. Be disciplined and determined. Above all, keep the joy in your experience.

FANfare

Management
Moka Musik,
14 Church Street,
Moncton, NB,
E1C 4Y9;
(506) 383-1483 (phone);
(506) 585-0871 (fax);
e-moka@staccato.nb.ca (e-mail)

Damsel in Distress

Some years ago I performed with a rather dramatic — if not down-right silly — bunch of musicians. The nightly antics required a number of theatrics and some fairly ridiculous costume changes. One evening, after the show I hurried out without bothering to change. The drive home was long and passed through some pretty remote country. As luck and a total lack of basic car care would have it, I was soon roaring along with most of my muffler dragging behind. Eventually the noise became annoying and I stopped to spend the next half-hour under the car, trying to free this unwanted appendage. This attempt proved unsuccessful, so I decided to seek help, as there were a few houses nearby.

It soon became apparent that the folk in this area were indifferent, and even hostile, to strangers, even to the point of sending a pitiful young female in distress off into the night. At last, one brave, albeit reluctant, soul came out and freed my car of its exhaust system. I called out to thank him as he quickly scurried off, scanning the area as if he was searching for my junkie boyfriend in the bushes. Undaunted but slightly indignant, I climbed back into my thundering vehicle and sallied on.

Arriving home I was greeted by my spouse's amused but rude remarks. I then caught a glimpse of a rather sad and macabre image in the hall mirror. A bizarre combination of grease, mud and glitter stared back at me, giving a first clue to my earlier chilly reception. There I stood, resplendent in a now-grimy red satin jacket and tattered running shorts with a pair of ancient army boots. This ensemble from hell was finished off with a splatter of green sparkle-paint eye shadow, with stick-on hearts and diamonds on a dirt-smeared face, complete with purple feathers crushed into a tangled mop of hair. Ahh, the joys of showbiz on a limited budget!

Barachois

The members of the French-Acadian quartet Barachois (pronounced "Bara-shwa") were born and raised on Prince Edward Island. Three of the four grew up together: Albert Arsenault and Hélène Bergeron are brother and sister, and Louise Arsenault is their close friend. Although Chuck Arsenault's Acadian heritage had been assimilated into the English culture, he describes himself as a "born-again Acadian." All are accomplished musicians, step-dancers and comedians.

The group has taken traditional Acadian songs passed down for generations and put their own signature on them. Their unique blend of high-energy Acadian music, dance and comedy appeals to anglophones and francophones of all ages.

Left to right: Louise, Chuck, Albert, Hélène

BOILY PHOTO

Music to Laugh and Dance To

Louise: Barachois is my family. We have something quite special in common. Because we spend so much time together, we have a closeness that you have with a family at home.

Hélène: The four of us worked together two summers ago doing dinner theatre. We enjoyed it so much that we decided to try to continue as a group. We gave ourselves a name: Barachois is that pool of water between a sandbar and the beach. But not just any sandbar; it has to be a big sandbar.

Louise: Our generation plays the traditional Acadian music we learned from our parents.

Hélène: Our parents are also great storytellers, very humorous. A big part of my upbringing was the clowning around. It's as much a part of the music as the notes or the songs or the names of the tunes themselves. That's what comes out when we play.

Albert: It's not too cerebral. It's more the energy, the liveliness we go for. If it's lively, we really get right into it. We can't close our eyes and just groove without our feet going, without a good rhythm going on the piano. Making music was always meant to entertain people and make them dance. We all dance. With dancing you have to be in the groove.

Hélène: I grew up in a musical family. I can remember my father playing the fiddle everyday. On Sundays, after Mass, he'd take out the fiddle and some of the kids would join him. One of my brothers had a cheap set of drums and we had an old guitar and a pump organ. We'd have big parties at my grandparents'. My grandfather and aunts and uncles step-danced and some sang. Dancing is something that I can't remember learning; it was just always there. The music was always there in my ears, too. It was just something that I took for granted.

opening notes

Albert Arsenault

Date of birth
August 11, 1964

Place of birth
St. Chrysostome,
Prince Edward Island

Current residence
Union Corner,
Prince Edward Island

Chuck Arsenault

Date of birth
April 10, 1969

Place of birth
Montague, Prince Edward Island

Current residence
Brackley Beach,
Prince Edward Island

(more ...)

FANfare

Management
House Party Productions,
P.O. Box 24,
RR#1,
Wellington, PEI,
C0B 2E0;
(902) 854-3019 (phone);
(902) 854-2167 (fax)

opening notes

Louise Arsenault
Date of birth
February 28, 1956

Place of birth
Mount Carmel,
Prince Edward Island

Current residence
Wellington, Prince Edward Island

Hélène Bergeron
Date of birth
October 27, 1954

Place of birth
Charlottetown,
Prince Edward Island

Current residence
Evangeline, Prince Edward Island

Heritage/languages (all)
We are Acadian, our mother tongue is French, and we are bilingual.

"This music has passed from generation to generation."

Louise: I also grew up in a musical family. My father played the fiddle and my mother played the pump organ. I started playing fiddle when I was seven. I've learned a lot of tunes from my dad. He used to take me to all the music contests when I was growing up.

Albert: My father never encouraged the kids to play the fiddle. He thought that, if you were going to play, you would pick it up someday. When I was around twelve, I asked him to fix me an old fiddle, and he did. His first lesson consisted of me watching his fingers as he played a tune twice around. Then he said, "Go to your room and practise." I would listen to whatever the rest of the family was listening to. My brother liked April Wine and Boston, a lot of the big American bands, rock, and rock 'n' roll. My mom also had a lot of records, the Carter Family and real country. She was a Nashville fan. But I was also listening to traditional and church music.

Hélène: We didn't grow up talking about being Acadian. We just were. We spoke French at home, and English when we left the area. We didn't learn about our culture in school. It's just in the last few years that we've been discovering a lot about our history. There's a lot of pride in one's culture; it's kind of a trendy thing nowadays to have a culture.

Albert: The more global the world gets, the more people want to stick to what's unique to them. And a lot of times it is the music. The music was always there; it's just getting to the public now. It went from the kitchen to the big stage, and now people are making money from it. If worst comes to worst, it'll just go back in the kitchen. Then it will just brew for a while until it comes back out.

Hélène: For our first album, a lot of the material was from field research that Georges Arsenault had done. He'd made recordings back in the 1970s of older women just singing into a tapedeck in their kitchens. This music has passed from generation to generation

discography

- **Barachois**/House Party Productions, 1996

— great, old Acadian music. Albert and I picked out some of the songs that had potential. Then we got together with Louise and made some primitive arrangements based on the influences from our childhood.

We've made music all of our lives. Career or no career, we'd do it anyway, we'd be playing music. It's not something that you choose. It is something that's a part of you.

Albert: There's still a little taboo about playing music for a living. People still ask us, "So when are you going to get a real job?"

Hélène: Some people say, "You actually get paid for going to play off Island? You actually get paid for these 'holidays'?" They think it's obnoxious to get paid for "having fun." Whether we are doing it for a living or not, we'd still be playing music.

Albert: We'd still be having the house parties and having a hoot.

MAKING MUSIC

Albert Arsenault
Saw, jaw harp, bones, fiddle, piano, feet, vocals, fork & knives, percussion

Chuck Arsenault
Suzaphone, trumpet, guitar, vocals, feet

Louise Arsenault
Fiddle, harmonica, guitar, feet, vocals

Hélène Bergeron
Keyboard, pump organ, guitar, fiddle, feet, vocals

Nothing Else Could Go Wrong

Hélène: We were doing a two hour show and were very anxious for things to go very smoothly since a well-known singer/songwriter whom we wanted to impress was in the audience.

At the end of the first set we patted ourselves on the back saying, "That went very well."

In the second set, all hell broke loose: Albert walked on his fiddle bow, snapping it in two; Chuck walked on his harmonica, flattening it beyond repair; and Louise broke a fiddle string in the middle of a tune. Grady, our manager, fled to the dressing room with Louise's fiddle to replace the string while I tried desperately to stretch out a song introduction. Suddenly over the sound system, to our horror, came the sounds of Grady plucking and tuning the fiddle, loud and clear, since the cordless on Louise's fiddle had been left on. We naively thought nothing else could go wrong as Albert got up to play a fiddle solo in a slow song. As he hit the first note we all cringed. The fiddle was hideously and hopelessly out of tune. We felt completely jinxed.

After that we thought it bad luck to play to impress rather than to have fun.

The Barra MacNeils

Members of the MacNeil family have been making music together their whole lives. By the age of ten, all were veterans of local and national radio and television. All are graduates of the music program at Mount Allison University, in Sackville, New Brunswick. Their self-titled debut in 1986 showed off impressive instrumental skills; then 1989's *Rock in the Stream* displayed their developing vocals, harmonies and songwriting. Several albums and ECMAs later, this dynamic family group are reaching international audiences with their unique blend of traditional and contemporary songs. The Barra MacNeils give us a timeless blend of past and present for every musical taste.

Left to right: Stewart, Lucy, Kyle, Sheumas

A Family of Music

Sheumas: We've played together since a very early age. Like most musical families in the Maritimes, we've evolved. Kyle and I started out at a young age playing at local concerts and community halls. Then we graduated and played at dances. Then the next thing you know, Stewart came along, and he started playing at the dances, then Lucy joined us. It's definitely a natural evolution — kind of like a big tumbleweed.

Lucy: I am the youngest in the band. My first summer actually performing full time was at Expo '86. It was pretty exciting going out to Expo and being with a lot of other bands. My brothers did a lot of groundwork, actually, before I entered the band.

Kyle: When we were growing up, we didn't really aspire to play on a world stage; it just kind of grew as we went.

Stewart: How we make music hasn't really changed since then. We still go out and collect traditional music and write music and receive songs from people. We still meet the same people we met years ago when we started out. They still come out to our shows. If anything has changed, it's the number of people we work with at the business end of it. I can honestly say that we still have a lot of fun making music.

Lucy: I grew up with music all around. That's all I really knew. I took lessons, went to university, studied music and have been performing since 1991. All of a sudden I just woke up and said, "This is pretty exciting!" It's easy to take it for granted. You're just going along and all of a sudden everyone from here is doing so well across the nation and internationally. You realize you can do something with this. You can go places and meet the most interesting people.

opening notes

Kyle MacNeil
Date of birth
April 21, 1963

Lucy MacNeil
Date of birth
October 24, 1968

Sheumas MacNeil
Date of birth
October 14, 1961

Stewart MacNeil
Date of birth
October 20, 1964

All
Place of birth
Sydney Mines, Cape Breton (NS)

Current residence
Nova Scotia

MAKING MUSIC

Kyle MacNeil
Violin, acoustic & electric guitar, mandolin, vocals

Lucy MacNeil
Vocals, bodhran, Celtic harp, viola, violin

Sheumas MacNeil
Piano, keyboard, vocals

Stuart MacNeil
Vocals, accordion, keyboards, whistle, flute, electric guitar

"It's music with a personality."

Kyle: Years ago, when someone asked what you did and you said, "I'm a musician," they'd say, "What do you really do?" Ten years ago, if you were promoting the East Coast and tourism and culture through your music and playing, they'd laugh at you. Now, it is the opposite.

Sheumas: The majority of the musicians in the Maritimes know each other in some way or other. No matter what group it is, the music is a thread that weaves through all of us. What strikes people is that the music is fresh. I guess it's just a family of music.

There are fragments of music from all over the world — whether it is Ireland or Scotland or New Zealand or Australia or the southern States. It's becoming more of a world of music. Even if you go to Africa now and start playing with somebody, you'll find tunes common to both parties.

We've played a lot of bizarre situations. We have played for huge audiences, in informal settings, formal settings, outdoors, indoors, tree houses, you name it. When you can walk away from the gig and say, "Hey, that was a good gig!" that's what keeps you going.

Lucy: When we're travelling I'm the only female. I'm surrounded by my brothers, the other musicians and the crew — all men. But growing up, I never had a sister. I'm used to my brothers and their friends always being around. In that sense I'm used to this world.

Some days it feels really good to have my brothers around, but it's hard on the boyfriend and can be hard on the nerves, the one I have left! It's comforting when you're travelling to know that there is someone always there. But sometimes it can be a little hectic.

discography

- **Barra MacNeils**/PolyGram, 1986
- **Rock in the Stream**/Barra Music, 1989
- **Time Frame** (re-release)/Mercury/Polydor, 1993
- **Closer to Paradise** (re-release)/Mercury/Polydor, 1993
- **The Traditional Album**/Mercury/Polydor, 1994
- **The Question**/Mercury/Polydor, 1995

Kyle: It's not just the traditional music that people come here for. People are coming to hear the different kinds of music that the Maritimes have to offer. It's just not traditional; it's the blues, it's jazz.

Lucy: There are a lot of East Coast musicians now, but we all have our own little flair, own little flavour in the music.

Kyle: Our motto has always been just to take it a day at a time. We've been at our music day after day, year after year, and it's been evolving slowly and steadily. It has never taken a step backwards. So as long as it's moving forward, we keep going with it.

Lucy: I love being from the East Coast and I love the music and the people and the food. It's music with a personality, fun, loving almost. And if you go away you can always come back. You can always come home.

FAN fare

Management
Phil Dubinsky,
51 Park Street,
Sydney, NS,
B1P 4W3;
(902) 562-3841 (phone);
(902) 567-1278 (fax)

Website
http://www.taisbean.com/Barras/

On the Road

One summer, a while ago, we were in St. Anthony on the northern peninsula of Newfoundland. We planned to take a flight at around noon the next day from Deer Lake to Halifax so that we could play in a folk festival the next night. When we realized that the flight connections weren't going to get us there in time, we got our flights bumped up to early morning. That meant that, after the concert in St. Anthony, we had to drive all night to catch the flight in Deer Lake. About midnight, we packed the gear in a bus, and we headed down in the fog. About six o'clock in the morning, near Corner Brook, just as we thought we'd make it in time, the bus broke down. There we were, about forty minutes from the airport, wondering what we were going to do. There wasn't a lot of traffic going by. Someone came up with the great idea that we should hitchhike to the airport. Well, no sooner did we start hitchhiking than trucks started pulling over. The side of the Trans-Canada was lined up with people wanting to help. We loaded all the gear up in the trucks and drove to the airport on time.

Now where else in Canada would you get people to pull over like that? It was pretty nerve-wracking that morning, but when we look back it was pretty amazing.

John Allan Cameron

CAROL KENNEDY

When fans of Maritime's "new wave" trace the musical influences of artists like the Rankin Family and Natalie MacMaster, they won't have to look long before finding John Allan Cameron. He was playing pipe tunes on the twelve-string guitar in the 1960's. He was a lone voice for the Celtic tradition, touring the country and hosting his own television show that aired first on CTV from 1975 to 1977, and then on CBC from 1979 to 1981. Stan Rogers had his first TV appearance on the CTV show, as did countless other Canadian musicians. John Allan Cameron became a household name in Canada. Today, ten albums and twenty-seven years later, he is not only their roots, he is also their peer. The music, like its "Godfather," has come full circle.

The Gospel of Celtic

When I was growing up in Glencoe Station, the fiddler and the priest were my heroes. There were seven kids in our family. I'm number two; one of the older lads. I have a brother ahead of me, John Donald. He plays the fiddle and teaches young people. My mother was very musical. On her side we are all related to Buddy McMaster and his people. Dan R. MacDonald, my mother's brother, was probably the most prolific writer of Celtic fiddle tunes in the world. The priest was also important in our lives because he preserved the traditions. I was in the seminary for seven years and was six months away from being a priest when I left. I went to St. Francis Xavier and Dalhousie, and then taught high school.

In 1964 I played at a Celtic concert in Glendale that Father John Angus Rankin held at his parish; it lasted for three days and included fiddlers from all over. A gentleman from CJFX Radio in Antigonish happened to be there. He taped my music and played it the next Monday on the radio. Within three or four minutes, he got about thirty calls to play that stuff again. That's how I got started, with CJFX Radio. When I was first starting, a lot of people would ask me why I was playing this type of music. I said, "Because it is an integral part of my soul and my being. You have to remain true to yourself." Now it has come full circle. A lady walked up to me last year at Louisbourg and said, "John Allan, I want to apologize to you for my generation, for not paying attention to you when you started." Another guy said, "You know what? You were right all the time, weren't you?" I said, "Yep. You guys are finally catching on." You can't deny the soul of the music. It's now being accepted worldwide. It's a bit of a phenomenon.

Back in the 1960s, when I was starting out, there was virtually no music industry. My management, which was Anne Murray's company, told me that, to try to carve out a career, you have to be where the action is. That was Toronto. One of Nova Scotia's greatest exports

opening notes

Date of birth
December 16, 1938

Place of birth
Inverness, Cape Breton (NS)

Heritage
Scottish

Languages
English, Gaelic, Latin

Current residence
Markham, Ontario

Instruments
Vocals, guitar, fiddle

> "You have to respect your audience."

was Anne Murray. She carried the music business on her shoulders in Canada for eleven years, before Bryan Adams, before any of them. I toured with Anne for five years. I opened her shows all across Canada.

You can have all the talent in the world, you can be a fine singer, a fine performer, but if you're not at the right place at the right time, with the right type of song and the right people in your corner working for you, it's like winking at a good-looking person in the dark. Sometimes it is more virtuous to go out in the foreign land and preach the gospel of Celtic to the unconverted, to people who have never heard it before. I remember stepping onto the stage of the Horseshoe Tavern on Queen Street in Toronto wearing a kilt. Now that's a country bar. Loretta Lynn played there, and all the big Nashville acts, and I arrived on the stage wearing a kilt! It took a certain degree of intestinal fortitude. But, as John Prine's song says, "You are what you are and you ain't what you ain't."

In the 1970s and 1980s, I played folk festivals all over Canada, and I always represented the Celtic side of Cape Breton. I also met a lot of wonderful performers through the festival circuit — people like John Prine, who became a really good friend. I think musicians have always gotten along very well. I respect every other expression of music. Every one of them has its own ontological goodness and transcendental pristine purity. Some people are better able to express it than others, but I totally respect people who go out there and give it their best shot, whether they are playing for a square dance in Prince Edward Island or a Cape Breton *ceilidh*.

select discography

- **Here Comes John Allan Cameron**/Apex/MCA, 1968
- **Minstrel of Cranberry Lane**/Apex/MCA, 1973
- **Lord of the Dance**/Columbia Records, 1977
- **Weddings, Wakes & Other Things**/Columbia Records, 1979
- **Free Born Man**/Glencoe Records, 1987
- **Good Times**/Freedom Records, 1990
- **Glencoe Station**/Stonecairn, 1996

They are doing something that is an involvement of their soul and spirit. To me that is the essence.

I love to perform. Some performers can't wait to get off the stage; to them it's just a job. To me it's a vacation. My job is to get out there and play and respect the audience. You have to respect your audience. The audience is the ultimate judge. They'll tell you whether you can stick it out or not. Longevity means that the public has said, "Yep, you're okay." The public will tell you if you're going to hang up your skates or not. It's important for young people to listen to the audience, to listen to what they are saying, and to have enough fortitude to go on ahead. My advice is to surround yourself with good folks and make a go of it. If it lasts ten years, great! If lasts two years, hey, you're at least skating on your end of the game.

It's time for us to pay more attention to the regions of this country, to listen to the people from Alberta, listen to the people from Newfoundland, listen to the people from Prince Edward Island and the Maritimes. There's a Latin phrase that means "behold how good and wonderful it is for brethren to dwell together in unity." That's my prayer for Canada. How can we stay united? Music is a universal language. Play music together, sing for one another.

FAN fare

Management
Rave Entertainment,
197 Charlotte Street,
Sydney, NS,
B1P 1C4;
(902) 539-8800 (phone);
(902) 539-9388 (fax);
rave@chatsubo.com (e-mail)

The Godfather, Part Two

Three years ago, at the East Coast Music Awards in St. John's, Newfoundland, my son, Stuart, and I were playing some Celtic guitar in our hotel room. A guy came in and said to Max MacDonald, "I hear that Ashley MacIsaac might drop in here tonight."

Max said, "Yeah, he might, but you see the guy sitting over there? His name is John Allan Cameron. If you want Celtic music, you listen to how he plays the pipe tunes on the guitar. He is the Godfather of Celtic music in this country."

"Oh, my God," the guy said, "is that Ashley's godfather?" The guy stuck around, but I don't know whether he listened to me or not.

Holly Cole

A. MACNAUGHTAN

One of the most exciting musical developments in recent years has been the emergence of Holly Cole. Halifax born and bred, Cole has carved a unique niche with her imaginative reworkings of standards, show tunes and contemporary songs.

Her natural register is a smoky contralto, but she can climb the heights with the cool, understated ease of a great jazz instrumentalist. In approaching a song, she doesn't rule out anything, emotionally or intellectually. In live performances, she combines the elegance and world-weary cynicism of the great German cabaret singers with the vulnerability of Piaf.

"5 1/2 out of 5 ... for both the silver-pierced and the silver-haired, Cole has something to offer."
— *The Winnipeg Free Press*

Canada's Own Sultry Jazz Diva

I'm a sixth- or seventh-generation Nova Scotian. My parents, who were both born in Halifax, met and studied classical music there. We've had Coles for many generations in Nova Scotia.

My maternal grandfather was born in Windsor, Nova Scotia. His land has been in the family since England stole it from the Indians. I never knew my father's father. My father's great-uncle was a singer and actor on Broadway. He did big shows like *The Boyfriend* with Sandy Duncan. My mother's family are Underwoods. My mom's father is a country-and-western accordion player. He is almost eighty-one, and he no longer performs, but he once performed on stage with Hank Snow — his claim to fame, and a pretty good one. We spent our summers with my grandmother and grandfather, and we'd listen to country-and-western music, show tunes and Broadway musicals. We sang all the time in the house. I just took music for granted. I started taking piano lessons when I was four. My parents listened to almost everything but jazz: mostly classical and traditional folk and Celtic music — no big surprise for Nova Scotia. I think you can hear those influences all through my music.

At school I was an oddity, an oddball. From ten to eighteen, I was completely into horses. It was my obsession. We had moved to Fredericton when my dad got a job with the CBC. We lived only a five-minute drive from the stable where my horse, Andy, was boarded. Every day before school, my parents would get up early and drive me there. I rode both Western and English. It was all competitive. I won seven trophies and fifty-nine ribbons. I toured. My horse is still alive. He lives in Paradise on the south shore of Nova Scotia. He is about thirty-two years old. My dream is to move back to Nova Scotia and live on the coast and have a horse.

I still go back the East Coast once a year. My parents are divorced now. My mother lives in Saint John and is the curator of a big

opening notes

Date of birth
November 25, 1963

Place of birth
Halifax, Nova Scotia

Languages
English, some French

Current residence
Toronto, Ontario

Instrument
Vocals

> "Having grown up in the Maritimes keeps me grounded."

museum. Since he retired, my dad lives half his year in Nova Scotia. My older brother, Allan, is also a musician. He's one of the people responsible for getting me into it. We were best buddies and still are. My little brother, Ted, is just figuring out what he wants to do. He's done a bunch of acting and singing, which is what I think he likes to do best.

When I was a teenager, my brother Allan went off to study music at the Berklee College of Music in Boston. At the time I was listening to music from the 1960s: Janis Joplin, Neil Young and Jimi Hendrix. I was a hippie wannabe. When he got back, he was asked to play in a band in Fredericton called the Martini/George Quartet. He mentioned to them that I knew how to sing. I can't believe he did it. I went to see them play and he called me up on stage to sing. It was brutal. I sang "Body and Soul." That was the beginning.

To that point my musical education had been pop music of my generation, a lot of rock and stuff I liked from the 1960s, classical music and Celtic music from Nova Scotia, plus a bunch of country and western, not new country, but the real twang, Hank Williams and all that.

Then when I was nineteen or twenty, I came to Toronto and enrolled in the Humber College music program. I went insane there. They wouldn't allow me to do what I wanted, which was to play drums as well as sing. Girls weren't suppose to play drums. To tell the truth, their attitude was just fuel for the fire in a way, because I took drum lessons on the side. But voice was my main thing. That was what I was there for, and I was rapidly getting to know what I wanted to do. I fell in love with jazz and plunged

discography

- **Girl Talk**/Alert Records, 1991
- **Blame It On My Youth**/Alert Records, 1992
- **Don't Smoke in Bed**/Alert Records, 1993
- **Temptation**/Alert Records, 1995
- **It Happened One Night**/Alert Records, 1996

That First Cry

I started to sing really young. My mother says that, when I was born, mine was the longest birth of all the kids. After however many hours, I came out and the doctor smacked me on the ass. A huge, deep howl came out of my mouth. He looked at her and said, "I guess you have a little alto here."

---

into it big time. I mean the pure stuff: singers like Sarah Vaughan, Ella Fitzgerald and Billie Holiday, the heavy-duty jazz singers. I didn't listen to anything else for two years.

Later I went back to some of the stuff I listened to before. Now my trio does a combination of things. My attitude toward music is entirely different than it was when I was younger and I immersed myself in pure jazz. I now believe there is room for traditional music. I love the traditional Gaelic, traditional jazz and traditional classical music. I think there is room for all of it.

Having grown up in the Maritimes keeps me grounded. It keeps things in perspective. It keeps me modest and humble. It also gave me a sense of humour. People [in the Maritimes] have a really good earthy sense of humour. It is definitely part of the music, and it is certainly part of my performance. I love to make people laugh, as well as do the really intense ballads, the dark moody stuff. It's great to make people laugh. That's part of my life and part of the show.

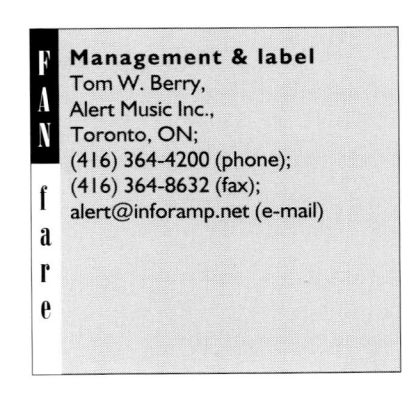

FANfare

Management & label
Tom W. Berry,
Alert Music Inc.,
Toronto, ON;
(416) 364-4200 (phone);
(416) 364-8632 (fax);
alert@inforamp.net (e-mail)

Stompin' Tom Connors

JIM FISHBACK

Over the past thirty years, the legendary Stompin' Tom Connors has been the voice of the average Canadian. Considered by many to be one of Canada's few bona fide folk heroes, he has travelled to every corner of this country and held firm to his beliefs, which include a strongly held patriotism, a hand extended to the underdog and an unflinching loyalty to friends.

Stompin' Tom has released an incredible forty albums. His latest, *Long Gone to the Yukon*, is his nineteenth album of self-penned songs. His autobiography, *Before the Fame*, is sure to bring us all to a greater understanding of Stompin' Tom.

Taking Everything in Stride

My mother was an unwed teenage mother. I moved more times in my first five years than most people do in a lifetime. My mother started us hitchhiking when I was three. Looking back, I can see that it must have been tough, being on the road like that, but it didn't seem that way at the time. For all I knew, every little kid in the world was travelling down some dirt road with his mother. To a little kid, what matters is having somebody to hold on to.

My mother gave me my love of music. She used to stand in front of the mirror with a broom for a guitar and play all the cowboy songs. When I was six, I was taken away from her and put in an orphanage. That was living hell. I ran away every chance I got. Then, when I was seven, I was adopted out to a farming family in Skinner's Pond, Prince Edward Island. I started writing songs when I was eleven. Actually, they were poems. I wanted to be a poet. But after a while I decided they'd sound prettier if I put a tune to them, and so I started doing that too. At thirteen I ran away from Skinner's Pond to work on the docks of Saint John.

Nothing changes with me. I'm the same yesterday, tomorrow, all the time. I still believe in all the same things. My songs never change, except I add new ones from time to time. But I'm still the same old guy and I take everything in stride.

I'm a lyricist more than anything, but when I write songs, the words and melody come together. The lyrical line comes first, then the melody for it, then another line and melody. I write on guitar. My fans come out for good entertainment. In my crowd, I have them from two years old to 102. Not everybody has that kind of crowd. I don't care if I make a million dollars. What I care about is how deep is the mark that I'm going to make among the people I write songs about. As long as they'll buy my records and get me a living, I'm very happy and I believe that's being successful. I don't write songs about this country for the money. My motivation has

---

opening notes

Date of birth
February 9, 1936

Place of birth
Saint John, New Brunswick

Heritage
Irish, French

Current residence
Southern Ontario

Instruments
Guitar, fiddle

> "My mother gave me my love of music."

more to do with the lack of nationalism in our country and the lack of songs about the heroes of it and the places in it and the work that people do. Canadians aren't spoken about in songs. I feel that's what we lack and that's what's wrong with our country right now. This country has been very good to the people in it, and it's about time we focus inside and realize how proud we should be of what we've got. If they would just play more Canadian music — and it doesn't have to be my music — our young people would wake up with a tune in their minds about Montreal or Vancouver, or some Canadian who has done some great deed. Folks ask me why I don't sing some of them nice Nashville songs. I tell them I'll be happy to sing some of them nice Nashville songs just as soon as them fellers in Nashville start singin' some of my songs, about my country! I left the music business in 1978. I stayed away for eleven years, until 1990, to protest the recognition that "border jumpers" were getting at the Junos. I sent my six Junos back then. But when I realized that the boycott didn't do a hell of a lot, I decided I might as well be back in the mainstream again.

What I see out there is something I've been wanting to see for so long. Even though the industry hasn't changed that much, the young people are making the changes. Hopefully I was instrumental in it a little bit. When I was given the Doctor of Laws degree from St. Thomas University in New Brunswick, I pretty near fell through the floor. When the press asked me what I thought about it at the time, I said, "Well, the best thing that I can think of is that it sends a great message to the people of the country — especially

select discography

- **Bud thd Spud**/EMI Music Canada, 1969
- **Stompin' Tom Connors Meets Big Joe Mufferaw**/EMI Music Canada, 1970
- **Stompin' Tom Connors Live at The Horseshoe**/EMI Music Canada, 1971
- **My Stompin' Grounds**/EMI Music Canada, 1971
- **Stompin' Tom Connors and the Hockey Song**/EMI Music Canada, 1972
- **A Proud Canadian** (compilation)/EMI Music Canada, 1990
- **Long Gone to the Yukon**/EMI Music Canada, 1995

to those with meagre beginnings, such as myself. It says that, if you stick to your guns and you fight for what you believe in, it might take a little while, but it pays off in the end."

I've hitchhiked across this country many times and held many jobs. Something that comes out of that is meeting a lot of people and knowing that the people in British Columbia are just the same as Maritimers, and Maritimers are the same as the people in Ontario and, back and forth, we're all Canadians. We're a hardy people, no matter where we're from, because of our climate. There's an awful lot of things that bind us together. When you learn those things by travelling the country, you get this intimacy with the country, and then not just Prince Edward Island is your home any more; Canada is your back yard, and everyone in it is your neighbour. And so that's how I became Canada-conscious. When I look at the mountains in British Columbia, "They're my mountains," like the fella said. I wouldn't give them up any more than I'd give up the docks at Skinner's Pond harbour.

FANfare

Management
Self

Promotions/orders
Rocklands Promotions,
P.O. Box 1586,
Peterborough, ON,
K9J 7H7

Website
http://www.emimusic.ca/tom

Highs and Lows

When my song "Bud the Spud" was a hit in Prince Edward Island, they gave me a parade in Charlottetown, with me perched on the back of a truck full of potatoes. The Minister of Agriculture gave me a gold-plated spud and thanked me for my contribution to the Island's potato industry. I guess I didn't feel like reminding them that the time before when I'd been in the city, I'd had to sleep in the jail because there wasn't anywhere else for fellas with no money.

J. P. Cormier

At the age of twenty-seven, J.P. Cormier has already lived a life that most musicians only dream about. He is equally adept at Celtic and country. He plays eight instruments and sings with virtuosity. He has played at the Grand Ole Opry, won the respect and support of stars like Waylon Jennings and Marty Stuart, toured the United States extensively and won dozens of fiddle, guitar and banjo awards. And now he has returned to the home of his youth, Cheticamp, Cape Breton. Since moving back to Cape Breton from Nashville, this multi-instrumentalist singer/songwriter has been very busy.

"I would be honoured to share a stage with him at any time."
— Waylon Jennings

Songs for the People

My roots are in Cheticamp in Cape Breton. My father and all my brothers and sisters were born there. But, by fluke, I was born in Northern Ontario. My father was a carpenter and was transferred there a few months before I was born. Then when I was nine, he passed on, and we moved back to the Maritimes. My father was also a tremendous fiddler, but, when he died, my mother sold his fiddle. I didn't learn to play fiddle until I was sixteen.

I grew up as an only child, since all my brothers and sisters were older. The brother next up from me is sixteen years older. I was really quiet at school, I never got involved in anything. I just stayed at home and played music. I started playing guitar when I was five. I performed all the time at home and for house parties. When I was a child, I didn't learn to read music, but I had this really bizarre ear. It was a gift from God. I could listen to a Chet Atkins song and in twenty minutes play it just like him. I lost that. Now I have to struggle.

My first performance was at the Ontario Central Exhibition right after Dad passed away. I competed and won against forty other guitar players. Then I started performing at bluegrass festivals. Once I got a taste of being on stage, I got addicted to it. I started learning everything I could by Doc Watson, Tony Rice and all those guitar players. I was fourteen when I did my first *Up Home Tonight* TV show in Halifax. That's when I realized that this was going to be my career. People I had never seen before knew who I was. That freaks you out.

When I was fifteen, I wrote my first song. It was called "The Chance," and it was recorded at the CBC. After that, I just kept writing. I've got about 300 songs now — all of them about life and most of them tragic. I write about things that matter to people. I like to write songs for fishermen and miners and police who don't have a voice. Lately I've been making up stuff, like the song "The

---

opening notes

Date of birth
January 23, 1969; Aquarius

Place of birth
Northern Ontario

Language
English

Current residence
Cheticamp, Cape Breton (NS)

Instruments
Guitar, fiddle, piano, mandolin, banjo, bass

"This is just the tip of the iceberg."

Molly May." It's about a man who loses a boat because he's old and a bit of a drunk. They give his boat to a younger person, who takes out the boat and sinks it fifty feet from shore. After I wrote the song, my wife, Hilda, told me something almost identical to that did happen in Cheticamp. I see it as symbolic of the whole fishery industry. The government has taken fishing away from the old men and given it to big corporations, and today they are ruining the fish stocks.

This place was pretty barren for musicians in the 1980s and right until 1991. There was no work here. In 1990 I put out the *Fiddle Album*. It was one of the first of its kind on the market to take fiddling beyond the usual piano-and-guitar accompaniment. There were drums and banjos and mandolins and weird arrangements and all of this different stuff going on. It bombed. It's a great album. People want it now, but then it was too far ahead. That just about finished me.

There wasn't anything going on except the CBC. The CBC kept me alive from 1988 to 1992. I got sick of driving a cab and doing security work and other things to make a living. In 1992 I went to the States. Then people started realizing how incredible the musicians here were. So in 1995 we decided to come home. At first I thought we were going to starve to death. I really did. I knew what it was like before. But since we got back, we have never stopped working. The climate is really different here now from what it was before. Though I haven't always lived here, my heart's always been here. There is a lot of music here by the water. There's something about this place that is incredible; it's a natural breeding ground for ideas.

People say that the East Coast music scene has exploded. I don't think it has even started, I think this is just the tip of the iceberg. There're some guys out there now who are amazing. If they

discography

- **Fiddle Album**/independent, 1990
- **Return to the Cape**/Main Tripp Records, 1995

ever get distributed in the Maritimes, and maybe overseas, they'll just rise right to the top. We're going to see an even larger move toward Maritime music, especially outside Canada, in Europe and the United States.

I'm playing with John Allan Cameron a fair amount these days. It's such a pleasure to play with him. He was my hero when I was a little kid. I thought he hung the moon and the stars. He was the first person I ever saw pick a guitar. It blew me away — especially since he was doing it with his thumb. I still can't get over that. The guy has a thumb like a bullet.

You have to stay humble. If you have talent, God gave it to you. That's the main thing to remember. That and not to hurt anybody playing music. Don't write stuff that's going to hurt people and don't sing or do anything to hurt people's feelings. The only way to gain experience is to go out on the road and just hang in there. We all need all the help we can get. Right now it is a crucial time, especially for traditional music. If we don't bring the next generation up, we could be in trouble. We need young people to start playing and to become interested in it. If they do, then we're unbeatable.

Fanfare

Management
Rave Entertainment,
197 Charlotte Street,
Sydney, NS,
B1P 1C4;
(902) 539-8800 (phone);
(902) 539-9388 (fax);
rave@chatsubo.com (e-mail)

Chasing 'Gators

I was on the road in Florida one time with Charlie Louvin from the Grand Ole Opry. We were staying at this guy's house, just killing time 'til our gig the next evening. Near the house was this large pond. Charlie decided he wanted to go down to see if he could find an alligator. He was in his late fifties then, a very slow-talking, relaxed kind of fellow. I went with him with a flashlight.

So, there we were, pointing the flashlight and looking for 'gators. Every once in a while Charlie would say, "There he is," pulling my leg. We'd get a little closer. "There he is," he'd say. All of a sudden I pointed the flashlight down right at our feet and we saw a big white mouth. I turned around and said, "There he is all right!" But when I looked, Charlie was already back to the house, almost at the door. I took off running too. That was my famous 'gator-chasing episode with Charlie Louvin.

Lee Cremo

Lee Cremo's great-grandfather, Michael, was given a homemade fiddle by one of the original settlers from Scotland and he learned the music of that era. That original fiddle was handed down from Lee's grandfather to his father, and finally to Lee. Hence, Lee's distinct style of Scottish reels and Irish jigs, mixed in with some Mi'kmaq traditional songs.

Lee is a noted composer of fiddle music as well as an accomplished musician on a number of instruments. The fiddle, however, is his first love, earning him the title of Maritime Canada Champion six times, and Best Bow Arm in the World at the World Fiddle Championship in Nashville, Tennessee.

Playing With Your Heart

I play mostly Scottish, Irish, French and Mi'kmaq music. My father was a fiddler. One day when I was seven years old, I grabbed a fiddle and tried to play a tune. It looked easy when everybody else was playing it, but it wasn't that damn easy. I kept at it, though. I practised and practised.

By the time I was about eight or nine, I was playing for the public. Then, one day, I heard Winston Scotty Fitzgerald and B.D. Wallace and Estwood Davison; they used to come into Eskasoni to play dances. If I heard a new chord, I'd ask someone, "What chord would that be?" We didn't have a piano in the house, but every time I was somewhere there was a piano, I'd try to find the chords. I played by ear until I was about forty-three, when I started to learn sheet music. You have to give me one round to hear how a tune goes, but if you give it to me a second time, I pretty well have the tune. Now, even when I'm not playing the fiddle, I always have a sponge ball in my hand. I squeeze it to strengthen my fingers. Or I'll pick up a cup, half-filled with water, with just my thumb and little finger, because you hardly use that finger.

I first recorded about 1966. I've recorded ten albums altogether. I've recorded for other people too. I especially help out other Natives. Some I hardly know, and some I know well. I helped Tom Jackson with his recording. And Willie Dunn and Bruce Cockburn. It was a good thing for me to win the ECMA, especially for my own tribe. The Indian is coming on strong now, but I was the first one who did it. Maybe the young people coming up will say, "If Lee can do it, then so can we." I try to encourage everybody.

The last song I wrote was when Elijah Harper fought for Native people in the constitutional talks. It was called "Constitution Breakdown." Everybody likes it. They are fiddling it in the Maritimes, in the States, everywhere.

opening notes

Date of birth
December 30, 1938

Place of birth
Chapel Island, Cape Breton

Heritage
Mi'kmaq

Languages
Mi'kmaq, English

Current residence
Eskasoni, Cape Breton (NS)

Instruments
Fiddle, guitar

> "If my fiddle is crying, you're going to cry with it."

Next, I am going to try out the fiddle with the bagpipe. I'll tune the fiddle in B-flat because most bagpipes are in B-flat. I don't know if it can be done, or if a soundman can cut out the drone so that I'll have the bagpipe but not that drone in the back. Bagpipes are very accurate. That's why Cape Bretoners are so good at the Scottish music. The music wasn't all written for the fiddle; it was written for bagpipes.

I also taught Natalie MacMaster and Ashley MacIsaac. I taught Natalie when she was about ten or eleven. Her mother used to bring her over here. Ashley's father, Angus, used to bring Ashley over when he was also about that age, too. I've taught others too. John Morris Rankin and his sister Rayleen used to sing for me. She was only about eleven then. I've been all over Canada and all over the United States, and I've been saying that if you want to find the good musicians, come to the East Coast. They are here — a dime a dozen.

I can't say that I never make mistakes in my music. People told me to straighten it out, but I don't want to. If it was meant for a mistake to be there, it's going to be there. I don't take shortcuts; I don't cheat. If I play something, my heart is there, even though my fingers or my bow arm might not be. I know I make some mistakes. But who doesn't? It's not about playing the music perfectly but playing with your heart. Don't condemn yourself for that.

Would you believe that I couldn't make a living in Cape Breton playing music? I had to drive a school bus for twenty-five years. But I was playing music every spare moment I had. Music is my first love. I think this music was a gift God-given to me. But I put a lot of work into it. Every time, before I play at a concert, I give a minute of silence to thank God that I'm still here and that the people enjoy what I'm doing. I'm not extra-special. God gave me only ten fingers. Everybody's got that. If you just put your mind and your heart to it, you can do it. When I play the fiddle, it doesn't

discography

- **The Champion Returns**/independent, 1995

A Standing Ovation

When I played at Expo 67 in Montreal, I didn't even know who Mayor Drapeau was. But, before I went on stage, I asked a guy in the stage area, "How much would you give me if these people give me a standing ovation?"

He says, "Mister, if these people give you a standing ovation, I'll tell my secretary to make you out a two-thousand-dollar cheque."

"Well," I said, "you're going to lose your money quick."

Then I got up on stage. I usually started on E-minor, but I told my piano player to go to G. He looked at me funny, because I never started in G and he didn't know what was coming. Then I started to play "O Canada," and everybody got up.

Yes, I won my bet and got my cheque. Then I found out the man was Mayor Drapeau! The piano player asked me later how I thought of that. "Well," I said, "just before we got to the stage, some girl from another country won something. They played her national anthem, and everybody got up. So I thought, why not play the Canadian national anthem?"

come from my fingers. It doesn't come from my head; it comes only from my heart. What's in my heart, that's what's coming out. If my fiddle is crying, you're going to cry with it. If you see my bow dancing, you're going to dance. My emotions come out in the fiddle. I believe that music is for the good of the community or the area you come from, and also for your own self, your own pride.

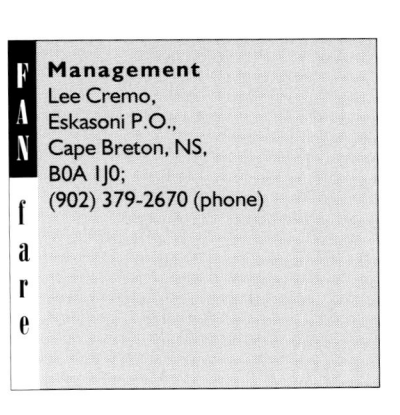

FANfare

Management
Lee Cremo,
Eskasoni P.O.,
Cape Breton, NS,
B0A 1J0;
(902) 379-2670 (phone)

Damhnait Doyle

ANDREW MACNAUGHTAN

Damhnait (pronounced "Dav-ven-net") Doyle is a woman with a firm grasp of who she is and what her music is all about. Overheard crooning in the office while working a summer job, she wound up with a record contract with Latitude Records. In addition to this bit of luck, Damhnait's wealth of talent brought her where she is today. Years of choral singing in the Holy Heart of Mary Chamber Choir in St. John's, combined with her spunk and natural grace, led to the recording of her debut album, *Shadows Wake Me*. The rave reviews keep coming as she steadily rises on the Canadian music charts.

"Hers is a flamboyant, expressive voice of tremendous power and clarity." — *Access Magazine*

Just Have to Sing About It

My mother comes from County Cork in Ireland, and my father from a place in Newfoundland called Avondale. He is of Irish heritage. My name comes from Ireland. My mother and father gave my brother, my sister and me unique Irish names. "Damhnait" means "fawn."

Until I was six we lived in Wabush, Labrador, where my father's family had moved to work in the mines. I used to share a room with my sister, and at night my mother would come in and play guitar and sing to us. My mother has a beautiful voice. When she was a child, she used to play the violin. My father and all his brothers and sister are very active in amateur theatre in Newfoundland and Labrador. I get a lot of my theatre background from him. My father is a professor now at Memorial University.

When I was six, my mother, who is a librarian, got a job in St. John's, and my immediate family moved there. I made my debut at a Christmas concert when I was in Grade Two. I came out in my little pyjamas and looked like a mouse. I sang "A Lullaby for Christmas Eve." I haven't stopped since. Later I sang in the choir of the Holy Heart of Mary, a Catholic high school. It was a chamber choir, and we sang a lot of sacred music, not because the school was steeped in religion —it wasn't at the time — but because it was beautiful music.

In my teens I listened to a lot of female singers/songwriters like Sarah McLachlan and Joni Mitchell, and to folksingers and the traditional music that is inseparable from Newfoundland. My mother listened to a lot of Irish musicians and I was greatly influenced by them. We listened to so much music, it's hard to pinpoint what exactly was the biggest influence. I mean, from Broadway musicals to folk to alternative, which my sister listened to, I really have had a huge, broad spectrum of musical influence.

I think about how it all happened for me every day. I know that if I hadn't been overheard singing in the office that day I would

opening notes

Date of birth
December 9, 1975

Place of birth
Labrador City, Labrador

Heritage
Irish

Language
English

Current residence
St. John's, Newfoundland

Instruments
Vocals, guitar

> "Newfoundland has so much to do with who I am."

still be singing now, I just don't know if I'd have an album out or if I'd be performing on stage yet.

I feel very fortunate to have had a chance to do what I absolutely love, but on some days I think maybe it would have been better if I had eased myself into it a little bit more, if I had taken three or four years and done the club circuit. As it was, when I started touring, I really hadn't played in public, and it was quite a shock to the system to go out and play every night. It was baptism by fire. It's like you're walking down the street and someone says, "Hey, can you do this?" and you go, "Yeah, I'm going to do it. This what I'm going to do for the rest of my life."

But now I'm really happy with how it's worked out. To go out as an opening act for a well-known band is really the best way to do it. In 1996 we were fortunate to do an East Coast tour with the Barenaked Ladies. I played guitar at some shows, but was not totally comfortable. I was still concentrating on getting my voice out there and working with the crowd, and I found it hard to do with a guitar. It's definitely an exposing thing to do, to play the guitar and sing when you're not used to it. But I'm working on that.

I always did a lot of writing — not necessarily lyrical or musical writing, but making up melodies in my head — but it wasn't until I was signed to a record label that I pieced it all together. I see myself as a singer/songwriter/performer. If I'm going to go out there and sing material in a band-type setting every night, I want it to be my own material. When I'm singing, I'm not just up there singing, I'm performing.

When I write a song, it's usually spurred by an emotion. Usually there's something going on in my life that I've got to express. If something is bothering me or making me happy, I have to write about it. It's not that I decide to write about quirky things or mundane things. My songwriting is a result of feeling miserable, or absolutely

discography

- **Shadows Wake Me**/Latitude Records, 1996

wonderful, and wanting to express it in some way, sort of to release it.

If I'm writing a song with someone, I'm not aware of the type or style of music. It's just that if what we are doing is good, if it's solid, that defines what type of music it is. It's not a conscious thing. If you pigeonhole yourself, then, when you try to break barriers, it's that much more difficult. I'd love to do a blues song or a folksong, but I don't think that should take away my loyalty or my integrity as a certain type of musician. I'm very open to different kinds of music.

Newfoundland and St. John's — the values of the place and the values of the people — have so much to do with who I am as a person. The people are so strong and wonderful there. It may not be evident in my lyrics, maybe because my music is not Celtic-based, but it's still there; it's inherent in who I am. It's such a huge part of who I am that it can't possibly not be translated into my work.

FAN fare

Label
Latitude Records,
49 Wellington Street East,
3rd Floor,
Toronto, ON,
M5E 1C9;
(416) 361-9264 (phone);
(416) 361-9241 (fax)

A Shocker

We were playing — I won't say where — in a bar with bad wiring. I was singing along, with my mike in one hand, and I was moving over toward one of my two guitarists. Suddenly I felt this rumbling all through my body. There were 500 people there, and I thought, "What in the world? One of the guys in my band must be shaking me. Why are they doing that?" Then I looked around and I realized there was no one there, and I screamed out in pain and in fear. I had this shooting pain up my left leg and out my right arm.

I turned to the audience and said, "I'm sorry, I just got the biggest shock of my life. I have to go backstage." I went backstage and realized I had just been electrocuted in front of all these people. We couldn't go back with the full band because it wasn't safe. So I said, "We've only done about six songs. That's a sin. All these people came out to see the show." So I went out with Cory, my other guitarist, who played acoustic guitar and I sang with no amplification at all. It was a big room. The audience all squeezed up front. They were really receptive. That was definitely my most shocking performance to date.

Teresa Doyle

You have only to attend one performance of Teresa Doyle's to experience the vocal power of this woman. From the Celtic roots of her native Prince Edward Island, Teresa's musical journey has taken her to Irish pubs, African villages, the Montreal jazz scene and Japanese concert halls. Her soulful and soaring soprano moves effortlessly from jazz to contemporary folk, worldbeat, Renaissance and traditional Gaelic music. She has recorded five albums on her own Bedlam Records label, the latest a refreshing children's album called *Dance to Your Daddy*.

"Doyle's vocals have a cutting edge and a projection as powerful as her song material." — *RPM*

Singing From a Place of Power

My family has been on Prince Edward Island for six generations. I am three-quarters Irish and one-quarter Scottish, and although I sing in Gaelic I don't speak the language.

My father is very musical, a traditional music fan and storyteller. He never played an instrument, but he "jigs" fiddle tunes — a form of Celtic mouth music. My grandfathers were musical, too. One taught me songs and the other paid me a quarter to sing them when I was three or four.

At university I studied political science and went off to the Yukon every summer to make money. I decided to spend a year in the bush there before going on to law school. One day I came into town for the Frostbite Folk Festival, which had an open stage. I sang a few songs and was invited to another folk festival in the Yukon called Farago. At the performers' party, I gave a rousing rendition of "Prince Edward Isle, Adieu" which I had learned for a political-science class. A guy came over to me and asked me to come to the Winnipeg Folk Festival. I didn't have a clue what it was, and I wasn't too excited. By the end of the weekend, I realized that the Winnipeg Folk Festival was the biggest gig in folk music in Canada, and the guy was Mitch Podolak, the director of the festival. Stan Rogers, who was also there, liked what I was doing. Later that summer I got to sing with him a couple of times in Whitehorse. These opportunities just came my way.

My writing is influenced by jazz and popular music. Historical characters fascinate me. I've collected many stories and write about people whose lives reflect some trial, event or moment of courage. For some reason most of them have been women, but the people who told me these stories were men. I don't know why they, rather than women, were the keepers of the stories.

I'm drawn to Celtic music by the storytelling and the traditional melodic structures. When I can, I improvise, bringing jazz phrasing

opening notes

Date of birth
January 26, 1957

Place of birth
Charlottetown, Prince Edward Island

Heritage
Scottish-Irish

Languages
English, sings in Gaelic but doesn't speak it, speaks French and Spanish badly

Current residence
Bellevue, Prince Edward Island

Instruments
Vocals, guitar

> "Having a child has been the best thing for my career to date."

and colouring to Celtic music. It's more centred in the heart and not as intellectual or sensual as jazz. Whereas jazz is urban, Celtic music comes from a rural, tranquil place. It's mystical and feminine. My Celtic music comes from a Stonehenge of my own.

Right now I'm hardly doing any jazz. I expect that, as I get older, though, when I have another decade behind me and another ten pounds on my hips, then I will be ready to sing some jazz. I've been blessed with a good instrument, and it's fun to take it to its outer limits. That's what scat singing is all about, and why it appeals to me.

Having a child has been the best thing for my career to date. It has brought me joy, humility, wisdom and a connection with another person. I think women come into their own in their middle years. My recent album, *Dance to Your Daddy*, is a collection of traditional songs that I chose for kids. I wanted to find Celtic songs that would bring kids into that kind of music. The lyrics are pretty tough, but that's okay: I learned those songs as a kid.

Here in Prince Edward Island, music is strongly rooted in the place, all mixed up in everything everyone does. As a kid I was exposed to a lot of traditional fiddle music, step-dancing and variety concerts. In other parts of the country, music is not as ingrained as it is here. Recently, though, Celtic music has become a worldwide, mainstream phenomenon. The Canadian music industry is looking toward the Maritimes, and East Coast musicians can now negotiate from a strong position. Many of us have built careers as independent musicians and created our own record labels.

Everybody benefits from the big successes that come out of the East Coast. Together we have created an industry from something that is part of our communities, not separate from them. It's

discography

- **Prince Edward Isle, Adieu**/Bedlam Records, 1987
- **Forerunner**/Bedlam Records, 1991
- **Stowaway**/Bedlam Records, 1993
- **Songs for Lute & Voice**/Bedlam Records, 1994
- **Dance to Your Daddy**/Bedlam Records, 1996

much easier to build a career now as an artist than it used to be, if you're from the boonies. Before, you had to move to Toronto.

The music business is difficult, but being in a stable environment helps balance a musical life. Being a mother is the most important thing to me right now. I spend a lot of time gardening, too. Whenever I'm feeling half a bubble off plumb, I garden. I don't know how good the music would be if I didn't have the other components of my life feeding it. There is a power in music. You take a melody, and people savour it and use it, pass it on, mould it, and a lot of energy gets built up. Music collects so much power over the generations.

FAN fare

Booking/management
Bob Jensen,
P.O. Box 3445,
Charlottetown, PEI,
C1A 8W5;
(902) 651-3281 (phone/fax)

Label
Bedlam Records,
RR#3, Belfast, PEI
C0A 1A0;
(902) 838-2973 (phone/fax)

All My Dues in One Night

Many musicians complain that they spent fifteen years playing the bar circuit, paying their dues. I figure I paid all my dues in one night.

It was about 1980, and I was playing in a little coffee house in Calgary with Scott Parsons. We had been playing there regularly for about four months. My cousins, who lived in Calgary, had never seen me perform, and this was the evening they were coming to hear me sing. I arrived that night to find the place was under new management. The new manager introduced himself and said that my partner and I would have to share the evening with two other acts. After the first set, we took a break and the second act was introduced. The second act was a stripper, and I thought that was pretty wild after singing these traditional Celtic songs. Most of the people were there to hear us and weren't sure what to think of this stripper stuck there between sets. After our second set, the new manager said he had very special guests, Mr. and Mrs. X from Cape Breton. They came out: he wearing a loincloth and she wearing a G-string and little tassels. They started collecting empty beer bottles from the tables and took them up on the stage and smashed them with a hatchet. My cousins were sitting up front, and my elderly cousin was called onto the stage to check that the glass really was sharp. First, Mr. X had Mrs. X lie on the glass and he stood on her belly. At the end of their show, he put a beer bottle between her breasts, blindfolded himself and hit the beer bottle with the hatchet, smashing the bottle without touching her. After the stage was swept, we came out and did another set of Celtic music. All the dues wrapped up into one night at a little folk club in Calgary.

Eagle Feather

J. Hubert Francis is the founder and leader of Eagle Feather, a Mi'kmaq group from the Big Cove reserve in New Brunswick. His music is influenced by rock, but at its heart are the traditional beliefs of his people. This mixture of new and traditional styles reflects the teachings of the elders, yet also encourages the aspirations of the young.

Two-time Juno nominee and East Coast Music Award nominee, the group has performed with Buffy St. Marie, The Good Brothers, Mickey Gilley and others. Wherever they go, the members of Eagle Feather are recognized as ambassadors of goodwill between the Aboriginal and non-Native peoples of Canada.

Following the Red Road

My parents and grandparents are all from the Big Cove First Nation community in New Brunswick. I was born and raised there, but my roots go back to a traditional gathering place called Beaumont, up by Memramcook, New Brunswick.

Eagle Feather has changed dramatically in the last four to five years. We felt we were trying too hard to be something else. We didn't realize that we had something unique, something nobody else was doing, or, for that matter, could do because most groups were not Native. So we began to write songs about our people, and to incorporate traditional chanting within our music. Much to our surprise, we came up with something that has been classified as Aboriginal Rock.

There have been some tough times for me in the past few years, times when I ask myself if this is worth it. But what keeps me going is my love for music. When you're fifteen or sixteen years old, you're looking for fame and glory. Now, that I am older and wiser, what matters to me is my responsibility to my people, the general public and myself. In my culture, there is a belief that you are given a gift from the creator, and whatever that gift is, it must be used to help others. That is your purpose in life. One of my purposes, I believe, is to sing and talk to people about my culture, my traditions and the philosophies of our ancestors. I hope that people will benefit from my work and get something worthwhile from the messages in my songs. We are taught that if you don't use your gift in a positive way it can be taken from you. There are not many people for Indian children and young people to look up to, people who can give them guidance and direction. I think that our Indian children need more Indian heroes.

My musical influence came mostly from my father. He is a fiddle player and he sings in a church choir in Big Cove. I began to play the guitar when I was about twelve. After my two brothers

opening notes

Date of birth
May 20, 1953

Place of birth
Big Cove Reserve,
New Brunswick

Heritage
Mi'kmaq

Languages
Mi'kmaq, English

Current residence
Big Cove, New Brunswick

Instruments
Vocals, guitar

> "Indian children need more Indian heroes."

dropped out of school, they went to work in Maine. They chipped in for a guitar, which they brought home and kept in our bedroom. When they left to go back to work, I took out the guitar and fiddled around with the chords I had seen them trying out. I started performing here on the reserve when I was about fifteen, mostly at birthday parties, particularly for girls. I eventually graduated to an electric guitar and played in a group. We started as an instrumental group because at that time nobody could sing! We did cover tunes such as "Walk Don't Run" and "Wipe Out."

In the late 1960s to the late 1980s a lot of stuff happened in my life — alcohol and drugs. I didn't play much music. I tried being a husband and a father but I was too busy partying. A few times I landed flat on my face. The last time I got up I felt that if I fell down again I wouldn't get back up. It was a very bad time for me. I started to feel that something was missing from my life. I had tried going to A.A. I tried rehabs. I tried religion. But a part of me was missing: my culture, my roots and my traditions. The proverbial light came on for me when I started getting into Mi'kmaq spirituality. I focused on the Mi'kmaq philosophies, visited the elders, began going to the sweat lodge and taking part in ceremonies. That was what was missing. It helped me and is still guiding me today. I've seen a lot of my friends die of alcohol and drugs on my reserve, and I am doing whatever I can not to let that happen any more.

Our tradition is called the Red Road by some. It means to go back to your tradition and follow it. You have a path that you must stay on. You can't jump on and off whenever you feel like it. It's a way of life and you must live it.

"Mother Earth," one of the songs on my last album, focused on what is happening with the earth, the hurricanes, floods, fires and wars. We feel that these are warnings that are being sent to

discography

- **Reverence**/independent, 1993
- **No Boundaries**/independent, 1994

us. They are Mother Earth's way of telling us we need to take better care of her.

Mi'kmaq is my first language, but I sing in English so that my message reaches more people. I sing about the teachings and the visions of our elders and our ancestors. My music is based on rock 'n' roll because of the influences I had back in the seventies. The biggest influence was a group called Redbone, a Native group from Las Vegas. I also sing ceremonial chants I learned when I came back to my traditional ways. I sing these in the sacred realm of the sweat lodge.

Recently, Eagle Feather was chosen as the New Brunswick representative to perform at the prestigious Lincoln Center in New York City. We brought a group of dancers with us. We performed a sweetgrass ceremony at the beginning to acknowledge the four directions and the four colours of people. We did this because we feel that people need to understand who we are, what it means to be a Native person, and what we are all about.

When the East Coast Music Awards began a few years ago, their main concern was promoting Gaelic and Irish music. Eagle Feather was not in this league. The only Native musician playing that type of music was Cape Breton fiddling sensation Lee Cremo. A few years later the ECMAs began to grow and eventually added an Aboriginal category, recognizing the talents of the Aboriginal people of the East Coast. We are currently talking about forming an organization for Aboriginal Maritime performers, musicians, dancers, actors, drum groups, etc. to promote our music and our people.

The Mi'kmaq have always been a nomadic people. To us there are no borders, no provinces, no country south of us. To us it's all the same land. We call it Turtle Island. Our Aboriginal music is universal. It is unique in that it has its own life. It is created by life's experiences. Aboriginal Music is about culture. It is about tradition and most importantly about our brothers and sisters.

FAN fare

Management
Brian J. Francis,
P.O. Box 7, Site 4,
Big Cove, NB,
E0A 2L0;
(506) 523-4116 (phone);
(506) 523-4901 (fax)

Four the Moment

Four the Moment is a four-woman a cappella vocal group from Halifax, Nova Scotia, that has been taking their brilliant music across Canada since 1981.

Uncompromising and beautiful, their compositions tell stories of Afro-Nova Scotian history, women and struggles in developing countries. Their music draws on the diverse and rich threads of Black music: blues, soul, reggae and gospel. The title songs for the nationally acclaimed NFB films, *Black Mothers, Black Daughters* and the musical soundtrack for the film *Them That's Not: The Feminization of Poverty*, were written and performed by Four the Moment.

"Four the Moment just get classier on every outing … their repertoire create[s] electricity."
— *The Mail-Star*, Halifax

Celebrating Community

Kim: My heritage is Afro-Nova Scotian. I was born in Halifax, but raised in the community of Lake Loon in Westphal, Nova Scotia.

Delvina: I'm also Afro-Nova Scotian and grew up in the community of Lake Loon, which was 210 years old in 1996. Kim and I are sisters.

Anne-Marie: My family is from Trinidad and Tobago. I came to Canada in 1972.

Andrea: My heritage is French Canadian, from Southern Manitoba, and I grew up in Winnipeg. I moved to Halifax nineteen years ago and now I've made it my home.

Delvina: At an anti-Ku Klux Klan rally in Halifax in 1981, a friend and I got a group of people together to sing. We were the precursor to Four the Moment. Then, the next year, at a women's benefit, my sister Kim, a cousin, Jackie Barkley (one of the original members of the group) and I got together and sang a song that we learned from an album by Sweet Honey in the Rock, an African-American a cappella group. That's when Four the Moment was born. A CBC producer heard us at a women's benefit and invited us to do a studio recording. We didn't have but one song, but we learned some others. As time went on, we performed at national folk festivals and wrote some songs of our own. Andrea's been in the group for twelve years. This particular combination has been together since Anne-Marie joined us eight years ago. Nine women have passed through this group.

We come from communities that emphasize justice and humanity, and we tend to write and sing about that. We're involved with the women's community, the Afro-Canadian community and on a number of community based and international development

---

opening notes

Delvina Bernard
Date of birth
November 8, 1958

Place of birth
Halifax, Nova Scotia

Kim Bernard
Date of birth
April 26, 1963

Place of birth
Halifax, Nova Scotia

(more ...)

Photo, clockwise from left: Delvina, Andrea, Anne-Marie, Kim

opening notes

Andrea Currie
Date of birth
August 23, 1960

Place of birth
Manitoba

Anne-Marie Woods
Date of birth
January 10, 1968

Place of birth
England

All
Current residence
Halifax, Nova Scotia

MAKING MUSIC

All
Vocals

issues. Our stories and songs reflect these communities we come out of.

Kim: Each one of us brings something unique to the group. In my sixteen years with Four the Moment, I've seen it change. It has been so great seeing people's reactions to the music and getting inspiration to write songs about experiences in our community.

Andrea: I grew up in a family that loved music. My mother was the first person I ever harmonized with. Before I joined the group, I was a fan of Four the Moment. I was drawn to the group's mix of a beautiful sound and commitment to community, and to telling stories that were not often told. Four the Moment is constructive and contributes to the evolution of all of us on this planet who are trying to get things happening in a better way. As the member of this group who doesn't share an African heritage, I feel that celebrating our differences is wonderful. We connect through our differences in a way that doesn't negate them, that doesn't minimize them, but that instead celebrates the richness of humanity, of difference. That's important to me.

Anne-Marie: I joined the group at a fairly young age and had to learn an entire repertoire in a short period of time. Being involved with Four the Moment has definitely helped me to develop as an artist. We have travelled to many places and seen how our music touches people in the audience. I remember one particular time in Kingston, Ontario when a young student gave me a poem he had written about Martin Luther King. Although we sang to hundrends of students, this student approached me because the music touched him and he wanted to share something with me that he had written.

discography

- **Still Standing**/Jam Productions, 1987
- **Four the Moment: Live!**/CBC Maritimes & Jam Productions, 1993
- **Four the Moment: In My Soul**/Jam Productions, 1996

Delvina: There are definite omissions with respect to the definition of East Coast music. The good news is that there are groups like us and the Gospel Heirs and Urban Renewal, and bands that play the jazz-and-blues clubs who negate this current limited definition. People like Bucky Adams have been carrying the torch for a long time and are constantly working to ensure that the definition of East Coast music is expanded. We want to claim our own space, speak in our own voice, sing our own sound. It's important to respect the music communities that exist here; we all deserve equal space and time. Unfortunately, the mainstream market is not always sensitive to the reasons people create music in a culture. Music is a reflection of people's lives. Some people in the East Coast music establishment are finally becoming more hip to this reality. For instance, the East Coast Music Awards will have a new category for Afro-Canadian musicians, which is a start. We in the community must also get involved with the industry, and use the resources available there to do things such as recording and touring. Walls and barriers have to be knocked down. East Coast music is getting lots of attention, but the attention is being paid to the music of the dominant culture. We have only begun to see what's happening on the East Coast. There's a lot more to it.

FANfare

Management
Jam Productions,
P.O. Box 31154, Robie RPO,
Halifax, NS,
B3K 5Y1;
(902) 443-6608
or (902) 490-6243 (phone);
(902) 490-6187 (fax)

"We want to claim our own space, speak in our own voice, sing our own sound."

How to Schmooze

We all get along so well. When we are out and about, people look at us and see how closely knit we are. We're always laughing together. When we get invited to something like an industry party, we mix and mingle and get to know other people. However, throughout the course of the evening, we end up gravitating toward each other. I guess you couould say we need schmoozing lessons!

Annick Gagnon

Annick Gagnon exudes charm, poise and talent. Anyone who has seen her in concert or on her music videos can sense her love of performing and her delight in the audience's rapt attention.

By age thirteen, Gagnon had opened for superstar Céline Dion. Since then, she has performed for thousands, including at the Canada Day concert on Parliament Hill in Ottawa in 1994. She has also managed to record three albums; study seven years of classical piano, dancing and singing; and enter university. Winner of the Best Francophone Recording at the 1996 ECMAs, Gagnon has her sights set on superstardom. Through the years, she has developed a naturally strong and wide-ranging voice.

"Gagnon is a tiny bundle of booming voice and dancing bop!"
— *Daily News*, Halifax

Going for an Adult Contemporary Market

I was born in northwestern New Brunswick in the bilingual town of Grand Falls/Grand-Sault, with Maine to the west of the Saint John River and Quebec as our neighbouring province. So you can imagine that we were influenced by both English and French cultures and the American culture as well. We receive more radio and TV programs in English than in French. That is probably why it is easy for me to sing in both languages. But we really have to make an effort to retain our French culture.

My family stretches way back in Grand Falls, New Brunswick. Both sets of my grandparents were raised here; the Gagnons were probably always here, and there are lots of us. Both sides are French speaking. I'm the first in our family to do the music thing. We listened to a lot of music in the house, but my parents don't play any instruments. My two sisters, both younger than I am, sing and dance. Sometimes we perform together.

Music began for me at about age ten, when I started to sing in my church choir. I was one of three soloists in the "Ave Maria." We had three mics, but since mine was the only one working, my voice was the only one heard. I guess it sounded pretty good. After that, it all began to snowball. I started voice lessons with Madame Edwina Lynch. We have worked together for seven years now. I recorded my first album, *L'Oiseau*, when I was eleven. I'm finishing up my seventh year of piano with the Royal Conservatory, but now that I'm in university, I think I might lay back a little from the piano and really concentrate on getting great marks. My manager, Michael Ardenne, is really important to me, together with the team that's backing me up: my band, my two sisters, who do back-up vocals, and also my parents, who give me all their support.

At home, we listened to POWER 96, now Q96, from Maine. I listened to Cyndi Lauper and Tina Turner. We always listened to a lot of rock 'n' roll. La Famille Simard are the only ones I

opening notes

Date of birth
October 7, 1978

Place of birth
Grand Falls, New Brunswick

Heritage
Acadian

Languages
French, English

Current residence
Grand Falls, New Brunswick

Instruments
Vocals, piano

> "Music is a difficult business to be in."

remember who were French. Besides that it was all in English. Perhaps that's the reason I am going for more of an adult contemporary market. I identify myself as an adult contemporary musician although I have, during the last seven years, performed many different sytles of music. I love the music and the style that goes with adult contemporary music and all the things you can do with the instruments. You can make a guitar sound really good.

My first professional CD was produced by Marc Beaulieu, Roch Voisine's music director. The title track, "River of Love," was composed by none other than David Foster.

I'm starting to write my own material, but I'm not used to it yet. It's a whole different thing. I have to keep in mind that I'm first a singer, not a writer. That's why I enjoy co-writing. I'm now attending St-Louis-Maillet, the Edmunston campus at the University of Moncton. I'm taking only three courses and I'm doing my music at the same time. I'm going for a DSS in medical science, but if my career should develop to a point where I could not handle my studies and my music, my first priority would be my singing career. Later, I would enjoy touring very much.

Music is a difficult business to be in. Being a professional musician means that you have to dedicate your life to living, breathing and sleeping music. It's very demanding because you're always in the spotlight. It also means endless hours of practice and repetition, day after day, without respite.

East Coast music defines us as a people, putting our personality, our way of living and thinking into evidence. In the Maritimes, people are very friendly. Our way of life is simpler and less stressful than in bigger centres, whether they be in Canada or the US.

When I'm in front of an audience, I can convey my feelings. The world is mine and in that moment I can do with it as I please.

discography

- **L'Oiseau**/independent, 1989
- **Malobiannah**/independent, 1991
- **River of Love**/ANC Music, 1995

A Bad Break

I was scheduled to sing in Bouctouche at Le Pays de la Sagouine one evening. I was waiting to go on stage with four other artists — we each had a little part to sing. I just had to go to the washroom in the worst way. When I came back, someone had sung my part for me. Apparently I came in too late. I went on stage anyway, but I didn't get to sing!

My motivation comes from my desire to succeed in what I love to do, sing!

My career highlight so far was the time I opened up for Céline Dion in Edmundston. I was thirteen then. She hadn't reached superstardom yet. She's a sensitive and warm person, really, really nice. I also had a great time at the ECMAs, especially winning Best Francophone Recording. Adult contemporary music is really a hard market to get into. If you're not determined, it's not worth it, but if you really want it, it's possible. You just have to work at it and keep trying all the time. That's the main criteria: keep trying.

FANfare

Management
Ardenne International Inc.,
Suite 444, World Trade &
Convention Centre,
1800 Argyle Street,
Halifax, NS,
B3J 3N8;
(902) 492-8000 (phone);
(902) 423-2143 (fax);
ardenne@fox.nstn.ca (e-mail)

Website
http://emporium.turnpike.net/
A/AAllen/events/ardenne.html

Lennie Gallant

GEORGE WHITESIDE

One of the musicians at the forefront of the East Coast music explosion is singer/songwriter Lennie Gallant. His albums have earned widespread critical acclaim as well as numerous awards and nominations from both the Junos and the East Coast Music Association. Gallant won ECMA "Song of the Year" award two years running, for "Which Way Does the River Run" (1995) and "Peter's Dream" (1996). Gallant writes and performs in both English and French. His songs have been recorded by artists throughout North America and Europe.

His resonant voice, innovative guitar playing and dynamic band have led to invitations to tour with artists as diverse as Céline Dion and the Crash Test Dummies, and to perform his work with symphony orchestras.

"An elegant, insightful talent."
— *Toronto Star*

Music from the Soul

I started writing songs at thirteen, as soon as I got my first guitar, and I've been doing it ever since. From the moment I had the instrument in my hand, it just seemed natural for me to put songs together. Throughout high school and university, I wrote songs, played and took gigs but I didn't feel that I could actually make a living at music. Later, however, I kept taking what I called "sundown jobs," ones that I knew would come to an end so that I could always go back to music. I eventually realized that music was what I really wanted to do, and I was just kidding myself by not diving into it full-time.

When I started writing, my heroes were singer/songwriters — Dylan, Prine, Lennon, McCartney and Lightfoot — some of my earliest influences. Also, when I was growing up in Rustico, there were always fiddlers around, but the music was more Acadian than Celtic. I later became fascinated by the energy and the melodic sense of Celtic music and by bands like the Bothy Band and Fairport Convention, and by the Celtic rock stuff that was going on in the British Isles.

I began playing with several Celtic bands like Speed the Plough, which I started with Roy Johnstone on Prince Edward Island. In that band, I began a musical relationship with guitarist Chris Corrigan, who introduced me to the music of Richard Thompson. Another band I loved playing with was Taylor's Twist — Kim Vincent, John Goodman and Rob Gordon — great Celtic players. We took some original songs and also a lot of traditional tunes from this region and married them to more contemporary sounds and rhythms. Even now, when I'm writing riffs for a song, I'm affected by the years I spent playing Celtic and Acadian music and quite often a Celtic rock number or two will end up in my live concert.

In 1989 I decided to release an album of my original material. At that time, there was not much of a recording industry here in the

---

opening notes

Place of birth
South Rustico, Prince Edward Island

Heritage
Acadian

Languages
English, French

Current residence
Halifax, Nova Scotia and Rustico, Prince Edward Island

Instruments
Guitar, bodhran, harmonica, mandolin, vocals

> "I always try to get right inside the song."

East Coast. So, I jumped into a Volkswagen with Janet Munson, my fiddle/accordion player, and Kevin Roach, a great mandolin/bouzouki/guitar player, and drove to Montreal. We got together with a bass player and a drummer the day before we went into a very inexpensive studio and recorded seven songs. CBC Halifax also helped a lot. They had just started a talent-development program in their brand-new studio, and I was able to record five of the twelve songs on the album there. That first album, *Breakwater*, because of my recent musical experience, had a Celtic tinge and a bit of a regional landscape to the songs.

The response to that album was very positive, and it got me invited to play all kinds of festivals and clubs across the country. Since then, I've been focusing on making a career playing and writing music. I've been fortunate in being able to do so. It's been an interesting journey and I find each new album somewhat of a marker, a departure point.

I like to think that the songs I write are true. I don't mean true in the literal sense but from an emotional perspective. I have to feel that I understand or have experienced the emotions on which the song or story is built. The setting may be from my own life, or things I've read, seen or heard from friends. Quite often it's a mix of these.

I feel I have a bit of a love-hate relationship with the blank page. I find writing an engrossing experience and there are times when I fear it, and will do almost anything to avoid it. (It's a good time for friends to ask me to help them move or something.) However, when I dive into it and the muse is generous, there is little that I find more exhilarating. I can become almost obsessed with creating the right marriage of music and lyric and with trying to hang on to the feeling I had when that first chord I hit released a

discography

- **Breakwater**/Revenant Records, 1989
- **Believing in Better**/Revenant Records/Sony Music, 1991
- **Land of the Maya** (cassette, benefit recording)/Oxfam, 1992
- **The Open Window**/Revenant Records/Columbia/Sony Music, 1994

couple of words or thoughts. I can spend a lot of time working on a song and it often has the curious effect of being very draining and energizing at the same time. Once in a while one will spill onto the page, word for word, in almost complete form. It's a gift when that happens. "Man of Steel," "Marie and He" and "Peter's Dream" were written like that. You almost feel like an interpreter when it occurs. You sure feel grateful.

In concert I try to play my songs from a very emotional centre. I also do songs that are just for fun, but if I'm playing a song that means a lot to me I try to get back the feeling I experienced when I wrote it. If I'm playing "Which Way Does the River Run," for example, I try to find a little piece of what I was feeling the day I wrote that song. I've heard some performers say that when they get on stage they often go on automatic pilot and think about the next day's drive or something. I always try to get right inside the song. I think the audience knows when you are really connecting with it.

What I find important here on the East Coast is a sense of community. We have been an almost-forgotten part of the country's music industry. For years people assumed that if you lived out here and you didn't move to Toronto or Vancouver, you couldn't be any good. That isn't the case. We live here because we want to; it doesn't have anything to do with the quality of the music or ability or talent. Success stories like Sloan, the Rankin Family, Ashley MacIsaac and the East Coast Music Awards have placed increasing attention on this part of the world and helped change industry perceptions. We still have a way to go, as there are artists and musical styles or genres that haven't yet received their due, but I think we've taken a giant step. This is reflected by the large number of recordings being made and studios that exist here now. It's an exciting time and place to be creating music and I'm glad to be a part of it.

I'm not much for giving advice, but I'll say this … if you feel that music is what you are meant to do, then do it. But don't do it to try and become famous or rich, or you're setting yourself up for a fall. If it's your passion, if it's in your soul, then you might make a living at it. Or you might not. But at least you'll be doing it for the right reasons. And that's the only kind of success that really means anything.

FANfare

Management
Pier 21 Management,
Suite 1701, 5151 George Street,
Bank of Montreal Tower,
Halifax, NS,
B3J 1M5;
(902) 492-2100 (phone);
(902) 492-3738 (fax);
pier21@fox.nstn.ca (e-mail)

Correspondence/information
Lennie Gallant,
c/o Revenant Records,
Hunter River RR#3,
Rustico, PEI, C0A 1N0

Website
http://www.chatsubo.com/Lennie/

Goodspeed/Staples

Halifax is thankful to claim ownership of Jeff Goodspeed and Dave Staples, two musicians who have devoted their lives to spreading the jazz gospel. Both came up through their high-school band programs, and in turn are teaching younger generations through programs like Acadia Band Camp and Nova Scotia Honour Jazz. Add to this a versatility and mastery of their instruments, and it is no surprise that they took away Best Jazz Recording at the 1996 ECMAs. Their recording, *Eastern Passage*, is a superb collection of ten original jazz tunes. The two are joined by well-known Halifax musicians Jamie Gatti and Tom Roach, and the result is a tight, fluid, East Coast-flavoured delight.

Jazz: The Ultimate Challenge

Dave: Ours wasn't the kind of family where you sat around the piano and someone grabbed the spoons. But there was always music around. My mother was a contralto. My dad sang and played some form of keyboard until he died. We lived in a small town outside Saskatoon, and there was a strong band program at the school. My two older brothers, who are now both music teachers, went into it, and I just followed in their footsteps.

I also played in rock bands in high school. It was 1970, and Woodstock had just come out. In the first band, I played trombone, but, in the second band, these guys had bought a keyboard and didn't have anyone to play it. I didn't play keyboard, but I taught myself. That band was called Nirvana.

Jeff: My mom and dad both sang in the church choir. I got my start in music because one day, when we were watching Don Messer, I pointed at the fiddle and said I wanted to play that. The next day I had one. I continued my violin lessons for five years. In Grade Seven I started clarinet and joined the school band. I was a little bit timid about carrying my fiddle anywhere — afraid to be teased or whatever. I went on to the clarinet because it seemed like a cool thing to do.

In school I was exposed to jazz through stage bands. To me jazz was always the ultimate challenge, improvising and composing on the spot. I think you participate in the music more as a jazz musician than perhaps any other.

Dave: Jazz is the logical place for a studying musician to go. I've always had an interest in jazz from playing piano; it's been natural for me to stay with it.

Jeff: Right out of high school, I went to Berklee College of Music in Boston for one year. Then I went to Acadia University, where I got my Bachelor of Music Education. Then I attended Humber

---

opening notes

Jeff Goodspeed
Date of birth
March 28, 1955

Place of birth
Halifax, Nova Scotia

Current residence
LaHave, Nova Scotia

Dave Staples
Date of birth
November 22, 1954

Place of birth
Saskatchewan

Current residence
Halifax, Nova Scotia

Photo, left to right: Dave, Jeff

MAKING MUSIC

Jamie Gatti
Bass

Jeff Goodspeed
Soprano, alto, tenor & baritone saxophone, flute, Irish whistle, EWI

Tom Roach
Drums

Dave Staples
Piano, keyboards, trombone

> "We realized it would be a great place for Sunday jazz."

College, where I didn't get anything except a lot of good experience and where I met a lot of good professional musicians. I moved around between Toronto, Nova Scotia and Ottawa for almost two decades, and then back to Nova Scotia.

Dave: I went to university in Saskatchewan and studied classical trombone and got my Music Education degree. Then I came to the Maritimes to teach. There's a good music program in the city schools here. It is unique, and that was enough to make me want to stay at the job. In 1991 I had a year off from school and travelled around the world. It was great to observe music and not play it. The experience piqued my interest in music forms I knew nothing about.

When I got back, Jeff was running a Sunday-afternoon jazz venue at the old Caravan Club here in Halifax. When it went under, the two of us went out for a drink to Maxwell's Plum and struck up a conversation with Darryl, the owner at the time. As we looked around the bar, we realized it would be a great place for Sunday jazz. Darryl eventually said, "Okay, let's try it." He tried us out in October 1992, and it soon became very popular, and a lot of people came down on a regular basis.

Jeff: Playing for years in the same club every Sunday, we've gotten to know each other really well. But there is also a community of jazz musicians in the area. I think playing with them as much a part of the gig as anything. Everyone comes through here at one point or another, and we get to play with everybody. It creates a little bit of a scene.

Doing the CD was a natural extension of that. We composed some of our own tunes and put them on tape. We certainly knew that Jamie Gatti and Tom Roach were going to be the two other guys in the Goodspeed Staples Quartet.

discography

- **Sunday Jazz Live at Maxwell's Plum**/CBC Maritimes, 1993
- **Eastern Passage**/CBC Maritimes, 1994

Dave: Nova Scotia is the right size to have a community in whatever kind of music you are dealing with. Some terrific jazz players have come out of this area of Canada. There's still a liaison between the people who went away and the ones who stayed.

Jazz is a kind of underground thing anyway. It exists right across this country and elsewhere. People play jazz whether there is a club in their city or not. In the last ten years, jazz has become mega-popular. Almost every major city in this country has a jazz festival now.

We and countless other people who have been teaching jazz in the Maritimes are starting to see the community grow. Our work with Nova Scotia Honour Jazz, which we co-founded, brings kids from all over the province together to study jazz for a couple of weekends a year. There are going to be a lot of young jazz instrumentalists coming up in the next ten years. It's still in its infancy in a way. But it's definitely becoming a tradition that was born in our school bands.

FANfare

Management
Jeff Goodspeed,
RR#1, LaHave, NS,
B0R 1C0;
(902) 471-4441 or
(902) 688-2755(phone);
(902) 688-1710 (fax)

Hit Those Keys

Jeff: Dave's electronic piano is a sampled piano, which means there are little recordings of a real piano and organ in there. The buttons that change the programs are located quite close to the keys on the piano. Dave had a little bit of a problem with it at first. Sometimes he'd be playing along and, all of a sudden, the piano sounded like an organ.

One time at Maxwell's Plum, Skip Beckwith, a great jazz player from here, was sitting in, playing on Dave's electronic piano. We were playing some nice peaceful tune, and Skip happened to hit the exact two buttons that it takes for the piano to start playing its preprogrammed demo song. All of a sudden this huge classical piece boomed out of the piano. Skip Beckwood pushed buttons everywhere, but he couldn't get it to stop. We laughed over that one, jazz colliding with synthetic classical at Maxwell's Plum!

The Gospel Heirs

The Nova Scotia-based Gospel Heirs have taken the gospel music, mixed it with rhythm and blues and added an element of 1990s dance music to produce a modern gospel sound that is original and powerful. The group believes that their coming together represents a wonderful opportunity to share the ministry of gospel music with audiences everywhere. All members reside in North Preston, Canada's largest Black community, and all attend St. Thomas United Baptist Church in their community. The Gospel Heirs recently celebrated their twentieth year as one of the most respected names in Canadian gospel music.

Back row, left to right:
Reggie, Rose, Alexander, Levi Sr.
Front row, left to right:
Burton, Wallace Sr., Levi Jr., Wally Jr.

A Gift from God

[Interview with Wallace Smith, Sr., group leader]

Our family on both sides has been in Nova Scotia for the past 200 years, but our roots go back to Africa. I grew up in a Black community called North Preston, about ten miles from Dartmouth. When I was growing up, the community was small and the church was small, but we had our own school. We would all gather on Sundays to sing in the choir and at Sunday school. There were nine children in the family: four girls and five boys. All the families from here are large.

My father, Oscar Smith, was a musician. Hank Snow used to work on a farm just down the road, and they used to work together. My father sometimes played with Hank at concerts and that. Dad had an opportunity to travel and play with Hank back then, but he never did. My father taught me to play the guitar when I was around six. I learned how to sing from a schoolteacher by the name of Reverend Doctor Fairfax. I also used to tap-dance a whole lot when I was smaller. My grandfather was in all kinds of tap-dancing contests, and he used to win a lot of them.

Most of our singing came from Sunday school and from sitting around the house after Sunday services and singing a bit of gospel music. I also played in concerts for school.

I started to play in a real band called the Rockin' Rebels when I was eighteen. I played lead guitar and did lead singing. The Rockin' Rebels played both country-and-western and Motown music. I had listened to a lot of country music: Gene Autry, Ernest Tubb, Conway Twitty, Elvis Presley. We got introduced to Motown through the radio. I fell into that and started singing Wilson Pickett and James Brown and some of the other ones.

I also sang in a band called the New Dimensions. We played everywhere, but this particular time, when it all started to change

opening notes

Wallace Smith, Sr.
Date of birth
July 29, 1942

Place of birth
Halifax, Nova Scotia

Heritage
Afro-Canadian

Current residence
North Preston, Nova Scotia

MAKING MUSIC

Reggie Coward
Keyboards

Alexander Fraser
Lead & background vocals

Rose Fraser
Lead & background vocals, piano, synthesizer

Burton Simmonds
Bass, background vocals

Levi Smith, Jr.
Drums, background vocals

Levi Smith, Sr.
Lead & background vocals, percussion

Wally Smith, Jr.
Lead vocals, back-up bass

Wallace Smith, Sr
Lead guitar, lead vocals

for me, we were singing at the Arrows Club in Halifax, down where the Metro Centre is now. Somebody had been talking to me about getting saved and using my music for the Lord. He told me that it was a gift that came from God.

I thought about it. I thought about changing my life for my family and giving them another hope in life. I was singing gospel music and playing other music too, but it wasn't working out. My children at that time would have been twelve, thirteen and fifteen. When I was playing in nightclubs and bars and dance halls, I'd look out and see my kids. I didn't think that it was fair for me to bring them up in that manner. I thought, "I don't have anything to lose. I'm not making any money anyway doing what I am doing, and I'm ending up with a lot of headaches the next day."

So, in 1979, I made up my mind to sing gospel music full-time. At that time there were nine of us in the New Dimensions. Levi Smith, Jr., Burton Simmonds and I left the band and formed the Gospelaires (later renamed the Gospel Heirs), and we've been playing strictly gospel music ever since. There's eight of us in the group now: two father-and-son pairs, a husband-and-wife team, a cousin and a family friend. It's a family group. Everybody is from the North Preston area, except Reggie Coward, who comes from Cape Breton.

I think it was the Lord in my life that made the difference. There hasn't been too much money, but I have received the blessings of other people through the ministry of singing. In 1981 I became a deacon in my church. Then, in 1990, the church gave me the opportunity to preach the gospel. Now I'm attending Atlantic School of Theology in Halifax to become a minister.

For me gospel music has the message of both salvation and faith, and it also tells me that there is life after death. The Gospel Heirs live by faith. When we go, we go knowing that God is with

discography

- **Free at Last**/Gospel Heirs Productions, 1986
- **In the Light**/Gospel Heirs Productions, 1992

us. That is the faith that keeps us going. Many people ask how we have stayed together for twenty years. We believe that God has joined us together until someone decides that they are getting too old and wants to get out of it.

We now do some contemporary gospel because we like to sing to the young people. Since they like to dance to up-tempo music, contemporary music, we have taken our gospel there, but we have not forgotten where we started. So we still do some traditional and spiritual songs like "Amazing Grace" and "Jesus Loves Me" for the older crowd. Our most recent album, *In the Light*, is all new material we wrote ourselves.

Our music is more rhythm and blues than anything; we got that from the Motown style of singing, and we haven't changed, but our music is unique because we want to make it our own from Halifax, or Nova Scotia, or even Canada, if you will.

In 1994 we decided to perform at the Queen Elizabeth Hospital's Christmas concert. At first we discussed using some other choirs. Then we said, "Why not make up our own choir?" So we asked our wives and our children and some relatives — everyone from four-years-old to fifty. Finally there were about thirty-five members, including some of the better singers here. We called it the Gospel Heirs Family Choir. The choir sang at the Black Cultural Centre in 1995 at the Christmas concert, and, in 1996, they sang at the Rebecca Cohn Auditorium in Halifax with us for our Gospel Heirs' twentieth- anniversary concert.

I don't think that we could ever repay the community for the way they have supported us. At every opportunity we let people know where we are from and who our greatest supporters are. We feel we have added to the community when we see the younger people getting into gospel music. A lot of young people are learning to sing and play different instruments, and they always ask how to get started and how to proceed. We try to let the young people know that there are spiritual gifts in life that will help you. Having faith certainly has helped us. They can see that over the years we've had to struggle, but we are still going on.

FANfare

Management
Eric McDow,
EMD Artist Representation;
(902) 434-7713 (phone);
(902) 434-2559 (fax);
emd@emd.ns.ca (email)

Website
http://www.emd.ns.ca/emd

"Gospel music has the message of both salvation and hope."

Great Big Sea

What started at a kitchen party in the Newfoundland fishing village of Petty Harbour has turned into one of the hottest bands in Canada. On *UP*, the quartet uses the mandolin, bodhran and accordion, among other things, to carry on the current trend of updating the traditional Celtic sound.

These four rollicking musicians keep their Newfoundland roots firmly planted and draw on the rock 'n' roll influences to attract ever-growing audiences.

"Enthralling, exciting, engaging. Everyone at the Great Big Sea show was at a party. There was dancing, there was laughing, there was toasting, and above all, there was music — beautiful, uplifting, unadulterated music."

— *FAX Magazine*

Left to right: Bob, Sean, Darrell, Alan

One Big Kitchen Party
[Interview with Alan Doyle]

We've always played music with a lot of energy. We listened to our folks play traditional folk music and, like any other thirteen-year-olds, we listened to KISS, Def Lepard, or Bryan Adams, and they always played with enthusiasm, energy and aggression. On top of that, we are all hams, and we love to perform. We all say we are performers before we are musicians. I'll always be like that. I enjoy playing music. When it comes time for a show, I want a big story to be told.

We all write a lot, but we're really critical of each other. We all wrote a few songs on the last record. I guess you write about things you know. And being twenty-something we write about being twenty-something. I've been writing a lot of songs about the uneasiness with commitment — mid-twenties stuff. "Do I have the right girl friend? Should I settle down? Should I buy a house?" Twenty-something questions.

We also sing some traditional songs and do some cover songs. But for us to perform an original piece, it's got to be the best that we can possibly do. It's got to be really good if it's going to stand next to "Lukey's Boat," which is, like, 390 years old. If it's not that good, we're not playing it. We are not the kind of band that says, "Okay, Ronnie just wrote a song so we're going to sing it now whether you like it or not." We are excited about playing every song. We want everyone to enjoy our music as much as we do. We are happy for all ages to come out to our shows. Some people want to sit in the back and relax and hear songs they heard twenty-five years ago. Some want to get halfway close to the front and dance, and some want to get right up close and yell and scream. I'm glad that we can offer a show that is ageless. I always want to do that. The music of Newfoundland kitchen parties was ageless. It wasn't just music for your grandparents; it was music for everybody. We want our shows to be like that.

---

opening notes

Alan Doyle
Place of birth
Petty Harbour, Newfoundland

Current residence
St. John's, Newfoundland

Bob Hallett
Place of birth
St. John's, Newfoundland

Current residence
St. John's, Newfoundland

Sean McCann
Place of birth
Carbonear, Newfoundland

Current residence
St. John's, Newfoundland

Darrell Power
Place of birth
Outer Cove, Newfoundland

Current residence
Pasadena, Newfoundland

MAKING MUSIC

Alan Doyle
Vocals, guitar, bouzouki, mandolin

Bob Hallett
Vocals, button accordion, tin whistle, fiddle, mandolin, mandola

Sean McCann
Vocals, guitar, bodhran, snare drum, tin whistle

Darrell Power
Vocals, bass

"The music of Newfoundland kitchen parties was ageless."

People all around the world love this roots music. It's people music. It's music that people sang while they were catching fish or while they were making bread or while they were going to their job in Dartmouth. The music has always been here. It's not a new phenomenon. There have always been wicked fiddle players in Cape Breton. And I hope there always will be. There have always been singers, songwriters, comedians and performers and there has always been Acadian music. All this wicked music is just finally being presented in a global form through CDs and cool packaging with cool videos and concerts with big light-shows. Kids who are fifteen are saying, "Wow, it's just as cool to be from Digby as it is from Brooklyn."

Ashley MacIsaac is the most exuberant. He's like a glam figure in Atlantic-Canadian music. But even Ashley said, "I'm only playing music that my dad taught me." It's just that we've all got a 1990s band and 150 lights and a big stage and explosions and special effects. But it doesn't matter if he has thirteen people with him or if it's just him and his cousin playing guitar or piano. It's still just songs and we are just singers. Music from the heart and from the kitchens leaves artists with a real down-to-earth feeling.

I was a teenager in the 1980s. My biggest influence wasn't Cape Breton or Scotland or Ireland or Liam Clancy; it was television. That was almost as big an influence as the songs my father and them were still singing. God bless them for still singing them. But East Coast music isn't only about playing fiddles and bagpipes. All the new interest has opened the doors for jazz acts and pop acts and the whole works.

If someone wants to become a professional musician, I'd say the same thing as to someone who wanted to be a plumber. If you want to be a plumber, be a really good plumber. If you want to be a musician, enjoy it and have fun. But don't be a musician because

discography

- **Great Big Sea**/Warner Music Canada, 1993
- **UP**/Warner Music Canada, 1995

you think your dad wants you to be a fiddle player. Finally, music is a logical career choice now for young people. It makes sense to want to be a musician now. The music industry has grown to the point that making a career in the arts is not out of the question any more. I'm always torn between two schools of thought about the music business and the music industry. This whole thing is like a boat ride. You can get on it and row hard. Then when it's over, you think, "I didn't enjoy that at all. All I did was row really hard and really fast." Or you can get on the boat and just lie there. But then the boat ride will be ten kilometres shorter than it would have been if you had rowed harder. Somewhere in between is a happy medium: enjoy the ride, but row it while you're at it.

Fanfare

Management
Quay Entertainment Services,
P.O. Box 843, Station C,
St. John's, NF,
A1C 5L7;
(709) 722-1991 (phone);
(709) 722-1839 (fax);
theguys@greatbigsea.com
(e-mail)

Fan club
Great Big Sea,
P.O. Box 152,
Station C,
St. John's, NF
A1C 5J2

Website
http://www.greatbigsea.com

Star Alert

We've had a million weird things happen to us on the road. This is one of them. We were in Toronto, staying at the SkyDome Hotel and doing a gig. It was around the time that the NHL Awards Television Special were in town. I've trained myself not to act like a weirdo when I meet a famous hockey player, and I was on "star alert."

Then, one day I was coming down in the elevator and the doors opened, and there was George Wendt, who plays Norm on the TV show *Cheers*. My brain is telling me, "Don't say something stupid. Don't say something dorky." I could have said, "Hello, Mr. Wendt, love your acting. I'm Alan from Great Big Sea in Newfoundland. Hope you can come see our show sometime." Instead as soon as the doors opened, I shouted "Norm!" at the top of my lungs.

The look on his face said, "Is that the best you could do?" It was rotten.

Bruce Guthro

JOHN RATCHFORD

Since winning the first-ever K94 Country Challenge in 1992, Bruce Guthro has been winning accolades from audiences and critics across the nation. The Sydney Mines native received a standing ovation for "Stan's Tune," the only original tune on the "Remembering Stan Rogers" tribute at Halifax's Rebecca Cohn Auditorium in 1996. Bruce's first album, *Sails to the Wind*, had a distinctly country sound, but recent pennings offer a broader appeal. Bruce is currently working on a new album that demonstrates a versatile and original songwriter with "a voice as soft as flannel and as light as air." (*Chronicle-Herald*, Halifax)

"Guthro is definitely poised to become the next Maritimer to break coast to coast."

— Paul Kennedy,
Halifax radio broadcaster

Being True to Yourself

Guthro is a French name, of course, a variation on Gouthro. My mother's maiden name was Boutlier. So we're French on her side as well. I tried to trace back the Guthro side. We are tied into the Roaches; that would be Tom the drummer, who plays with Goodspeed/Staples, and as far as I can figure we are tied in with Lennie Gallant's people from Rustico. There's got to be some Scots and Celtic in the woodpile somewhere as well. I grew up mostly in Sydney Mines, Cape Breton. There were nine children: the eight boys in one bedroom, and the one girl in the other. We grew up in an old house. There were never any two teacups that matched, and, if there were, if we were that lucky, there were definitely no handles on half of them. Before you took the cup down to pour your tea, you always looked in it first to make sure the old man's teeth weren't floating in it! We had a big floor furnace that heated the house, and in the bathroom we had one of those big red heat lamps. Three or four kids got in the bathtub at the same time.

There was always a variety of music in the house, from the Animals to James Taylor to Jim Croce to Pink Floyd. We listened to the radio, but, to tell the truth, my folks didn't have a whole lot of time to listen to anything. We did sing and play, though. The whole family sang at festivals. My grandfather played the fiddle. I remember him playing "Pop Goes the Weasel" when we were kids. We grew up two streets over from the Barra MacNeils. Whenever they had a party, they'd give us a holler and we'd go over and tell jokes and sing.

When I graduated from high school, I headed out west to work in a hard-rock mine. Later, I came home, and then went back out again and ended up in a place that had an old guitar lying around. It had only three strings, but I picked it up and started to dabble with it. When I came home, I had saved enough to buy a new one. My family thought I was crazy to buy one, but I had to. As soon as I got the guitar, my song writing started to bloom. I sat in the living

---

opening notes

Date of birth
August 31, 1961

Place of birth
Sydney Mines, Cape Breton (NS)

Heritage
French

Languages
French, English

Current residence
Sydney Mines, Cape Breton (NS)

Instruments
Guitar, vocals

> "We need music to lighten up our day."

room and picked away. Since I didn't have anyone to teach me and I didn't know enough about the guitar to learn other people's songs, I started to write my own. It was the best way for me to learn to play guitar, but I was still a living-room musician.

Then a couple of guys in local bands convinced me to go to these songwriters' circles and jam sessions. One night I got up and did a couple of tunes. Later, friends asked me to join a band they were throwing together. That was the first band I was ever in. I played the local club scene for a while and had fun and paid a lot of dues. Then I started to write songs. After that things just evolved. My career has been a steady climb, and that's the way I like to take things, slowly. I don't want to take off and start flying tomorrow because the fall would be a lot harder then. I'd rather keep my footsteps very firmly planted and remain more confident with what I'm doing. You have to be clever and realistic to make a living as a songwriter. For example, if I want to be true to myself and write an album full of ballads, I should expect it that it might not sell through the roof.

I don't have a clue what makes me write music. I just know it's where my passion lies; it's an inner thing. I was a serious daydreamer in school, constantly drifting and thinking about emotions and philosophy and what makes us tick.

My first recording, Sails to the Wind, was a country album. My new one has much more of me in it and the influences I grew up with. I grew up around Celtic music; I love Celtic music. On the other hand, most of the bands I played in were country and light rock/pop. That's what the clubs wanted to hear and the kids wanted to dance to. I survived on that for a long time. Right now I'm searching hard for a direction and my own sound. Eventually you have to stop copying others and just go after who you feel in your heart you are.

We all have different musical influences. I can't imagine anyone coming from just one vein of music. By working those different

discography

- **Sails to the Wind**/independent, 1994
- **Album pending**, 1997

Early Songs

When I went to high-school dances, a bunch of us would gather in the local woods and sit around a campfire, singing Stan Rogers songs and sea shanties. When we ran out, I tried to write tunes. We called ourselves the Brown Street Country Club. We had jackets and numbers and everything. It lasted all through high school.

---

styles into what you are doing, you can make music that is clever and interesting and commercially successful — and still be true to yourself. It may take me a few albums to evolve, to define who I really am and where I want to take my music.

Proud — that's what I am of the East Coast music scene, very proud. The world is now learning there is a strong movement coming out of the East Coast and it's good stuff. With the economy the way it is and the world in the shape it is, we need to tap our toes. And we need music to lighten up our day. We Maritimers are used to struggling for a job or migrating out west to look for work. I think music is one of the ways we've persevered, and maybe the rest of the world is getting a taste of that now.

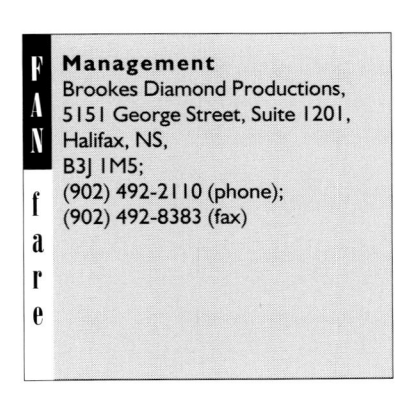

FANfare

Management
Brookes Diamond Productions,
5151 George Street, Suite 1201,
Halifax, NS,
B3J 1M5;
(902) 492-2110 (phone);
(902) 492-8383 (fax)

Ron Hynes

IVAN OTIS

Ron Hynes began his career on the coffee-house circuit in Newfoundland. In 1978 he co-founded the Wonderful Grand Band, a unique slice of Newfoundland music and off-the-wall humour with members of the comedy group CODCO. He went on to write for and star in *Hank Williams: The Show He Never Gave* and the *Opry Show*. Nominated for five ECMAs and one Juno award in 1994, he went home with three ECMAs, including the prestigious SOCAN "Song of the Year." His latest CD, *Face To The Gale*, paints a picture with music and gives the listener a short story come to life.

"A masterful fusion of pop, country and folk influences ... one of the year's best." — *The Journal*

A Love of Songwriting

I've been a gypsy all my life, but I now live in downtown St. John's which is where I am the happiest. I've loved songwriting since I was nine. I was always totally fascinated by it. There wasn't always a lot of music in the house other than radio and television in the 1950s. And in those days you're talking John Cash and Marty Robbins. Some guys in the community sang and owned guitars, and one guy in particular played Buddy Holly and stuff like that. I was fascinated by all of it. I am still influenced by music I hear today. If you stay tuned and alert, your style changes all the time.

I had an uncle on my mother's side. His name was Thomas O'Neil and his nickname was Sonny. Sonny sang and played, and was a country-music fan. His life is the basis for my song "Sonny's Dream." Everyone who has picked it up has brought a little of themselves to it. Lots of people have recorded it: Mary Black, Dolores Keane and Christy Moore in Ireland. Emmylou Harris has covered it. Here it's been covered by the Grand Band, Valdy, Terry Kelly, Evans and Doherty, and John McDermott. It's been popular in the U.K., and in other countries as well: Portugal, Germany and Japan. I've talked to buskers in Sweden who do that song. It has the status of a folksong, but it never had the status of an American hit. It's the one thing that it's lacked. In its twenty-year history, it's never had a major American release. All good work that stands out and has any kind of impact is removed from the artist. That's how it lives on: it has its own life; it perpetrates its own existence. That's what "Sonny's Dream" has done. It was really important to me to record an updated version of that song on my new CD, *Face To The Gale*.

To make a living as a songwriter, you have to write material and get it covered. The only way to make money is to get your work covered by people who sell a lot of records and/or get a lot of radio air play. That's the name of the game.

---

opening notes

Date of birth
December 7, 1950

Place of birth
St. John's, but raised in Ferryland, Newfoundland

Heritage
Irish, English

Language
Newfinese

Current residence
St. John's, Newfoundland

Instruments
Vocals, guitar, keyboards, mandolin, banjo

> "Break-up songs are the most fun to write."

I've co-written with Murray McLauchlan and Joan Besen from Prairie Oyster, and a few other people but I've probably co-written with my wife, Connie, more that anyone else. Songwriting with Connie is great, very rewarding. We were together for a number of years before we realized we could write together. The first song we wrote together was based on an idea that Connie had. It's called "I Never Met a Liar (I Didn't Like)." Joan Kennedy covered it, and it got to be number one in Canada right away. That was a real incentive for us. Now pretty well everything we write together is Connie's idea or her title. We have written a few break-up songs. They're the most fun to write about.

I love writing with women because you get in touch with that feminine side. Connie and I are in the middle of another project called "11:11 — Newfoundland Women Sing." It's eleven songs that she and I have written for eleven women artists, mostly from St. John's, and but from other parts of the land as well. It's a labour of love.

Maritime music is the most indigenous Canadian music. We don't have as much of an American pop influence on our musical heritage as, say, central and western Canada does — or even Quebec, which is the other part of the country that definitely has its own music. Both Quebec and the Maritimes have a heritage to draw from. That is what's unique about us down here. We grow up with traditional music, and whether we like it or are ashamed of it, influences what we do, and it influences what we try to create. It's what we are, the sum of where we came from. And you don't have to be an

discography

- **Ron Hynes: Discovery**/Audat/World Records, 1972
- **The Wonderful Grand Band**/independent, 1979
- **Wonderful Grand Band: Living in a Fog**/Grand East Records, 1981
- **Small Fry: The Ron Hynes Album for Children**/Sound Ventures/Islander Records, 1987
- **Cryer's Paradise**/Atlantica/EMI Music Canada, 1993
- **Face To The Gale**/EMI Music Canada, 1997 release

Irish fiddle player. You might be a jazz trumpeter, but your music will still have a little piece of Maritime flavour to it.

It was inevitable that the recording industry would come to this region at some point or another. There's just so much strength here, and it's so different from the rest of the country. But the impetus came from the Canadian music industry. I don't think that we suddenly made a big stride in a community awareness, or that all of a sudden everybody got better at what they were doing or got better press.

I remember seeing Rita MacNeil at Mariposa in 1972. She did a whole show a cappella, all by herself. She stole the whole weekend, as far as I was concerned. It was the most perfect show I ever saw. Not a band member on stage, not a musical note played. Everything was performed in its rawest form. Truly amazing. But no one was looking in this direction then. Years ago it was pointless to live in the Maritimes and hope to become a professional in your chosen career. You had to go to Toronto or Vancouver or L.A. There was no industry here. These days, communications being what they are, you can manage a career from almost anywhere in the world. You just have to travel and tour once in a while if you want to sell records.

FANfare

Management
Rosalie Goldstein
P.O. Box 31003
Winnipeg, MB,
R3B 3K9;
(204) 888-9470 (phone);
(204) 896-6033 (fax);
rocknros@magic.mb.ca (e-mail)

Website
http://www.emimusic.ca/

No Luck at All

The very first time that I ever played in Ontario, I had to play this gig in a bar way out past the airport. There was only one patron in the bar, but the bar owner made me play the whole night anyway, until about two o'clock, because he was paying me thirty bucks for it. The one guy in the bar was an ex-RCMP officer, and he was really drunk. In addition, the entire time I was on stage, there was another drunk pounding at the Exit door. Every time I was on stage playing, he kept pounding. At one point I asked the owner to let the guy in, but he said no, he'd been barred too many times. The owner didn't mind him pounding on the door. He just didn't want him in his bar.

At the end of the night, it was too late for me to get a bus home, so I started hitchhiking, and the drunken ex-cop picked me up. Halfway back to Toronto, he got pulled over by the police. They put him under arrest, and I walked the rest of the way home, probably twelve or thirteen miles. That was one of my earliest gigs, and one I'll never forget.

jale

CHARLES PETERSON

Four women met, discovered they could harmonize, divvied up who would play what, and in 1992 jale (an acronym of their first names) was born. Jale soon became the hardest-working band in Halifax, practising sometimes seven nights a week and working days to cover their equipment costs. Several years and recordings later, all their hard work has paid off, and a new constellation of jale has emerged, with original drummer Alyson MacLeod stepping out and Mike Belitsky stepping in. Their most recent release, *So Wound*, shows off a foursome that has matured as songwriters, musicians and performers, and has discovered an impressive knack for intricate harmonies and creative wordplay.

Defying the Labels
[Interview with Laura Stein]

When we first started, some of us were at art school and some of us were thinking about going to art school and some of us had just graduated. The music and arts communities intersect in Halifax, so we all knew each other. We just decided it would be a good thing to do — to get together, play music and try something new. We called ourselves jale after the first letters of our four names: Jennifer, Alyson, Laura and Eve. (Later Alyson left the group and Mike joined.)

At the time there were only a few women doing the kind of music we were doing, and we got a lot of support from people who wanted to see more women on stage playing. We had no idea what we were doing. We were just thrashing around on our instruments. That has definitely changed; I find it a lot more satisfying to be able to control the music. I like making a song seem really tight. I enjoy practising; we have a good time.

We've been given a lot of labels: "girl group" was popular when we started, so we'd get labelled as that. Our first tour we were labelled "riot grrls," which we're not at all. We don't have that kind of hardcore feminist content in our music. The second time we went out, people were talking a lot about "cuttle core" and lumping us in with bands like Cub from the West Coast. We got compared to the Go-Go's and the Bangles, but didn't get compared to a lot of bands that we listen to a lot, like the Pixies and the Breeders. Now that we have Mike in the band, people tend to label us as part of the mixed-gender groups. People really want to be able to slip you into some kind of category. You can't escape it unless you're in an all-guy group. If there is any female in there, you will get labelled as something.

We all write songs. It's fun to express ourselves in a song and then make a full band arrangement. There are differences, however. Eve likes recording and doesn't enjoy playing live so much.

opening notes

Laura Stein
Date of birth
May 3, 1967

Place of birth
Montreal, Quebec

Heritage
Jewish, American, Irish

Languages
English, French, a bit of Spanish

Current residence
Halifax, Nova Scotia

Photo, standing: Eve; **front, left to right:** Jennifer, Laura, Mike

MAKING MUSIC

Mike Belitsky
Drums, percussion, vocals

Eve Hartling
Guitar, vocals

Jennifer Pierce
Guitar, vocals

Laura Stein
Bass, vocals

Alyson MacLeod (left group in May 1995)
Drums, vocals, guitar

"Just be brave and do what you want to do."

I find recording much more stressful and enjoy playing live. Maybe we complement each other that way. Jennifer usually deals with heartbreak in her songs; hers are the saddest ones. Mine are also quite personal, but maybe a bit more vague. Eve shies away from anything very personal and concentrates on a subject or a phrase.

For a lot of the time that we have been together in the band, we have also been in school, and doing different things, and have had different priorities. We are now finally converging on something that we all want to focus on. We are becoming self-sufficient as musicians. Our influences have changed quite a bit, too; different things have come to the fore and others have gotten left behind. Our most recent record, *So Wound*, is very different from our first one. I don't think we'd be able to repeat ourselves if we tried.

Working in the group has been an interesting experience. There are a lot of compromises to make because we all have different visions and ideas. Different elements come into play, and ideas get mixed around. In the end, what we each come up with influences us again. Things do change. For a while we thought the band would be over when Alyson left because we had identified ourselves as four individuals. But we were lucky to find Mike, who is a really good drummer. And he's willing to work in the way we do, to say, "Okay, if that's the way you do it, I'll work that way too."

We feel pretty separate from other groups that aren't rock 'n' roll and pop. I don't feel real connections to them. We did play on

select discography

- **Aunt Betty** (3-song 7")/Cinnamon Toast, 1992
- **Sort of Grey** (2-song 7")/Derivative/Cinnamon Toast, 1993
- **Gold Leather with Heel Detail** (2-song 7")/Genius/Cinnamon Toast, 1993
- **Dreamcake** (12-song CD/cassette)/SubPop, 1994
- **14 08 93** (2-song 7")/SubPop, 1994
- **Closed**/Murderecords, 1995
- **So Wound**/SubPop, 1996

Ashley MacIsaac's first CD, but Ashley is so much at the crossroads of different kinds of music that he is able to bring lots of things together at once. The fact that he can do that is incredible. Otherwise we are pretty much an entity unto ourselves, and I think the rest of the East Coast views our music as different, and not the real East Coast thing. We are also signed to an American label. The only labels that approached us were American. We didn't have any interest from Canadian labels at all. The interest in East Coast "alternative music" really started only when Sloan got signed to an American label. That put a lot of focus on the kind of music that we play, but other music — especially Celtic and traditional music — has become really popular as well.

Our band has been so lucky to have had support from the beginning from people around us. We just opened up and started to do what we wanted to in the public realm. That's a really big step, and probably the hardest one: to just be brave and do what you want to do.

FANfare

Management
Murderecords,
P.O. Box 2372,
Halifax Central,
Halifax, NS,
B3J 3E4;
(902) 422-6114 (phone);
(902) 422-2194 (fax);
af797@ccn.cs.dal.ca (e-mail)

Looking the Part

Our record *Dreamcake* was doing really well in Britain and our label, SubPop, was anxious for us to come over there. England is such a flash-in-the-pan place; you really have to hit it at the right time. People in England really liked our record, and I think they had this image of us being these sort of sleek pop stars with a real attitude and a way of dressing. We, however, gave no thought to stage grandeur. We hadn't been playing much together, and our personality and stage presence were a lot more ragtag than now.

Our first show in London was opening for L-7, a hard-rocking, all-women heavy-metal group. We opened up with our little ragtag thing, wearing sneakers and blouses. People threw beer bottles and cans on stage, and we got trashed in the British press for not being glamorous enough. The critics said we looked like teachers. Later, to try to make fun of the whole thing, we dressed as teachers at a photo shoot. We put on glasses and blazers and stood outside some Gothic columns. It worked for us; we laughed a lot. But I'm not sure if anyone else got the joke.

Roy Johnstone

Roy Johnstone truly celebrates and communicates the pure joy of music and movement. He integrates the best of Prince Edward Island's traditional fiddle styles with classical, blues and jazz influences. Whether playing a slow air or a wild dance reel, his music is a voice that speaks to the heart.

Roy began classical violin studies with the Canadian Conservatory of Music in Winnipeg. During his teen years, he played guitar in several rock 'n' roll groups. In 1978 he moved to Prince Edward Island, where he joined the Queen's County Fiddlers and, together with Lennie Gallant, founded the popular Island group Speed the Plough. His fourth release, *Stark Ravin'*, received two nominations at the 1995 ECMAs.

An Islander from Winnipeg

In the late 1800s, my four grandparents emigrated from Scotland to Canada. They spoke a bit of Gaelic, but there was no traditional music or fiddling in my upbringing. When I was about six, I started studying classical violin at the Canadian Institute of Music in Winnipeg. I remember the Saturday-morning bus rides to my fiddle lessons downtown, all the other kids with their hockey gear and me with my fiddle. Despite the jokes and ridicule, I hung in, although I was doing my weekly lessons more to please my mother than to please myself. At that time, I really didn't have any understanding that music could be a form of personal expression.

When I was about fourteen, I bought an EKO guitar and was immediately invited to join a rock 'n' roll band. We practised in the garage behind our house. The band was a lot of fun. Playing at sock hops and school dances was a good way to meet girls, but the violin wasn't too popular or sexy, so it was relegated to the bedroom closet.

University was basketball, fraternity parties, physics and math, no music! I graduated and began my Masters in computer science at the University of Manitoba. My father worked for the airlines, so I could fly anywhere free as a student. I travelled in the Middle East and Turkey, and visited Cuba a few times. On these trips, I would search for the local music and often purchased traditional instruments and brought them back to Canada.

Then I got a job teaching at Argyle Alternative School. I was hired to teach physics and general sciences but the program was very open. Anything the students wanted to learn about we tried to teach. I taught photography, film and video, environmental studies and music. We had a lot of the best blues, jazz and folk musicians coming to the school to do concerts and to give workshops. We had some great jam sessions!

opening notes

Date of birth
July 9, 1949

Place of birth
Winnipeg, Manitoba

Heritage
Scottish

Language
English

Current residence
Argyle Shore,
Prince Edward Island

> "Fiddle music is an incredibly powerful stimulant for building community."

My work in alternative education and my interest in environmental studies brought me to Prince Edward Island to visit the Ark project and the wind test site in 1977. I fell in love with the place and the people. I moved here the following spring and bought fifty acres of land in Millvale.

In Prince Edward Island, Lennie Gallant was a major influence on me. We performed for a while as a duo, Lennie and Roy. The response to the guitar and the fiddle and to Lennie's writing was really positive, so we just kept playing. The band expanded and we formed Speed the Plough, with Sigrid Rolfe playing whistle and flute; David Papasian playing violin and cello; and Margie Carmichael writing, singing and playing guitar.

I joined the PEI Fiddler's Society and became an Islander by adoption. I feel connected to this place and the music. The sense of community and my friends are a big part of why I've stayed. Traditional fiddling gets a lot of support here, so it's been financially good. I can make a modest living in Prince Edward Island playing fiddle, and I like the lifestyle. There's the freedom and opportunity to be creative and somewhat independent and yet there's a strong and supportive community if you need help.

Fiddle music is an incredibly powerful stimulant for building and maintaining community. At a *ceilidh*, a house party, there are people of all ages — kids, grandparents and old-time fiddlers — who play music. I wasn't born here and I didn't grow up here, but when I play the familiar tunes I can see their faces light up. The old tunes are a living history for them and they bring back memories which people share with me. I'm very grateful to be part of continuing that tradition. Other music — jazz and blues — interests me, but there is a limited market for that music here.

discography

- **Rolling Waves**/independent, 1990
- **Them Times with David Weale**/independent, 1992
- **Flying Tide: When Strikin' a Stone**/independent, 1992
- **Roy Johnstone Stark Ravin'**/Fiddle Head Productions, 1994

I'm drawn to Irish music. I love to play airs and laments. The pieces are slower, and many are in a minor key. The Celts were an emotional people, and their music has a sense of lament for things lost. It's a culture that expresses grief openly, celebrates it and doesn't try to hide it away. Most of the players on Prince Edward Island are influenced by traditional Scottish music and many don't even play minor tunes. In Scottish music there's more of a lift, a drive that makes it suited to dancing.

People look to music to raise their spirits. It gives them a real sense of joy and celebration. I think people are searching for a sense of connection with traditions and cultures that went before us. At the same time, there's the dynamic process of people trying to create new sounds, not in a vacuum, but through what they have experienced. I'm trying to find more ways to create my own little niche where I can express myself and feel as though I am growing musically, and where I can give something back to the community from which the music came.

FANfare

Management
Fiddle Head Productions,
RR #1,
Bonshaw, PEI,
C0A 1C0;
(902) 675-2541 (phone/fax)

Tall Tales

About five years ago I was asked to do some children's shows for Spinnaker's Landing up in Summerside. I had studied a bit of theatre with the Bread and Puppet Theater Company from the United States and I had learned how to make a pair of stilts. I thought perhaps I could fiddle on stilts and it would be my claim to fame; I'd be the tallest fiddler in the Maritimes. The first show I did was a Canada Day celebration. The kids were so amazed by this ten-foot-tall, skinny character playing the fiddle that they all raced at me and started banging into me. I realized I could easily fall, that the kids could topple me over. Luckily my partner got them away from me. At another show, in Mill River, Prince Edward Island, I had the stilts strapped on with canvas. I was right in the middle of the second act, fiddling away and dancing up a storm. I danced onto the lawn while the kids were prancing around, and all of a sudden the canvas ripped and I just crashed to the ground. Because I landed sitting, everybody thought it was part of the show, so I fiddled to the end of the tune. After that I retired the stilts.

Mary Jane Lamond

From traditional "milling frolics" to concert stages, Mary Jane Lamond is taking the country by surprise. Her haunting melodies and richly textured sound help breathe new life into a long-forgotten art.

Her unique voice is featured on "Sleepy Maggie," from Ashley MacIsaac's recording *Hi, How Are You Today?* She has won prizes at the Gaelic Mod in Ontario, performed at the Isle of Harris Festival in the Hebrides and select U.S. events, and toured across Canada. At the 1995 East Coast Music Awards, she was nominated for Female Artist of the Year and Roots/Traditional Artist of the Year for her Gaelic record *Bho Thir Nan Craobh*.

DEREK SHAPTON

The Gaelic Minstrel

I grew up all over the place. My mother is from Halifax, and my father is from Albert Bridge, near Sydney, out in the Mira area. He was an engineer and we moved every few years, but I spent every summer down in Nova Scotia. My parents used to refer to going to Nova Scotia as "going home." It was where all my family was. In other places we didn't have cousins and aunts and uncles. Nova Scotia always seemed the place where we belonged. We loved to go to Nova Scotia, and I always wanted to live there. My mom's family, the MacDonalds, were from Hants County. Grandfather was a businessman who moved from there to Halifax. The MacDonalds arrived in Nova Scotia from the United States as early as the 1780s or 1790s, after the American Revolution.

"Lamond" is an Anglicization of the Gaelic name MacLaomuinn. My father's grandparents spoke Gaelic, and I got interested in it after learning a couple of phrases from my grandfather. Hardly anybody from the Sydney area in my father's generation learned any Gaelic. They didn't teach it in school; it was considered something older people had.

In the evenings, my mother played the piano and sang old folksongs, and I loved to sit and sing with her. As a child I was in choirs and took piano lessons. I was brought up on folk music. My mother listened to Peter, Paul and Mary. She played classical music, as well. Later on, there was David Bowie, and I got into punk. My whole life I have been into alternative music, never mainstream music. I was never passionate about pursuing any music until I got into Gaelic songs, which, I suppose, are another kind of alternative music in today's world.

I remember as a child being fascinated by Gaelic music. I didn't pursue it much until I was living in Nova Scotia and learned a couple of songs phonetically in choir situations. Then I encountered some traditional singers in Cape Breton. I was at a milling

---

opening notes

Date of birth
November 5, 1960

Place of birth
Kingston, Ontario

Heritage
Scottish

Languages
English, Gaelic

Current residence
Inverness County,
Cape Breton (NS)

Instrument
Vocals

> "Gaelic songs are another kind of alternative music."

frolic — a traditional Gaelic singer's gathering — and the music sparked me, so I went back to school to study Gaelic. Once I started learning about the folklore and meeting Gaelic speakers from Cape Breton, I got more involved in the culture. It became all-consuming. Partly it's a roots thing, but it's also so interesting, and the people and the music are great. You become part of a community.

My music career happened unexpectedly, organically. The first time I performed at the East Coast Music Awards, record-company people asked me about my career plans. I thought, "I sing Gaelic songs. I'm not going to make a career in the music business." I wanted to do a PhD in Celtic studies. As graduation day approached, I was invited to tour with Ashley MacIsaac. It was a job and I didn't have one, so that's what I did. Like many things in my life, my career just happened. Sometimes I wonder if that's the best way to live.

My new album is experimental in terms of Gaelic music but is not heavy rock the way Ashley's is. I'm going to call it *Suase!* When people are singing a song or playing a tune at the milling table, they yell this as encouragement. Literally it means "up with it," or, in Cape Breton vernacular, "go for it." It's a combination of the traditional and a new twist.

Gaelic music is about people sharing knowledge and songs, an exchange, and it doesn't happen in a performance. As soon as you get up on a stage in front of a microphone, you've lost the communal aspect of the music. The music is only one part of the culture. I thought about different ways I could try to communicate the culture, perhaps with slides, because whatever I do on stage is not a fair representation. I had already taken a step outside the tradition, and felt apprehensive about performing the music. Finally I decided

disco graphy

- **Bho Thir Nan Craobh (From the Land of the Trees)**/B&R Heritage Enterprises, 1994
- **Suase!**/Turllemusik/A&M, 1997 release

to do the best I could to perform the music creatively, although creativity is not what is cherished in Gaelic tradition which is why Gaelic songs have survived so long.

Whatever happens to preserve Gaelic has to happen at a community level. All I can do is sing in Gaelic and try to support a community of people. I'm therefore getting more involved in projects at home. One project is a co-op to support *Am Bráighe*, a newspaper focusing mainly on Cape Breton Gaelic culture which Francis MacEachern puts out from Mabou. I hope that, if this next album is successful, I can help fund that project. The higher my profile and the more albums I sell, the more influence I have for consciousness raising. My success has all fallen in my lap, so now I see it as an opportunity to give something back to the community.

I was surprised when my first album *Bho Thir Nan Craobh (From the Land of the Trees)* was nominated for the East Coast Music Awards. I wondered who was going to listen to an album all in Gaelic. But that album has done well. People like Natalie MacMaster and Ashley are very successful right now, and basically they play Cape Breton fiddle tunes. I sing only in Gaelic, and that has become accepted. Working with Ashley and seeing kids just bopping and having mosh pits to the music, I think it's cool that this music is from their own country, from Cape Breton. To be able to rock and have a mosh pit to traditional Cape Breton fiddle music is pretty extraordinary. But then, Cape Breton fiddle tunes are dance music, after all.

FANfare

Management
Jones & Co,
5187 Sackville Street, 2nd Floor,
Halifax, NS,
B3J 1K5;
(902) 429-9005 (phone);
(902) 429-9071 (fax)

Language Difficulties

I remember performing at an exhibition in Nova Scotia with Ashley. I got up on stage, and I explained that I sang in Gaelic. After the show, a woman came up to Gordie Sampson, who was playing guitar with us, and said, "You boys were just wonderful."

He thanked her, and when the woman continued, "That singer — " Gordie cut her off and said, "Isn't she great?"

"No," she said, "she has a pretty voice, but I couldn't understand a word she was saying!"

Ray Legere

Raymond Legere is becoming known as one of Canada's premiere fiddle/mandolin players. He has toured with Tony Rice throughout the New England states, with Michelle Shocked throughout Australia, Canada, and the United States (including Carnegie Hall), and with Alison Brown, who opened for Richard Thompson in California and Western Canada. Raymond currently performs on his own as well as with Terry Kelly, John McDermot and Cape Breton's Brakin' Tradition. He has recorded on hundreds of sessions and currently has four projects of his own.

Bluegrass by the Sea

I'm Acadian. My dad is from Cap-Pélé, New Brunswick, and I was born in Amherst, Nova Scotia, where my mom grew up. We lived in Ingonish, Cape Breton, for about a year and a half and in Moncton, New Brunswick for some twenty years, until I moved back to Amherst four years ago.

Since we always associated with English-speaking children in Ingonish and Moncton, I don't speak much French. Actually, my dad changed the last name on our birth certificates, but on his there's no "e" on the end of Legere. When Dad and Mom got married, they stopped speaking French altogether.

The music comes from my father. He was a multi-instrumentalist — a fiddler player, a mandolin player, the first five-string banjo player in the area — and he also played saxophone, clarinet and drums in school bands. His mother always wanted him to play old-time fiddle tunes and waltzes like Don Messer did. She wanted me to get started on the fiddle, too. My dad thought the fiddle was a difficult instrument to start on, so he bought me a mandolin when I was ten. Dad showed me some chords on the mandolin, which is tuned the same as the fiddle, and then I started picking up some melodies from old-time fiddle records.

In 1979, my uncle, Ronnie Leger, took me to my first bluegrass festival, where I was blown away by the musicianship of the mandolin players. They were improvising like jazz musicians, making up solos as they went along. I realized you can really do a lot with a mandolin, so I started practising with tapes of the Bluegrass 4, the popular bluegrass band from Moncton, learning to improvise instead of playing the same notes every time. One Christmas I got some records by American bluegrass bands. They could really play and did some extraordinary things on the instruments.

On the advice of my parents, I took two years of electronics in community college, and then went to the States to try to make a

opening notes

Date of birth
September 20, 1965

Place of birth
Amherst, Nova Scotia

Heritage
Acadian

Language
English

Current residence
Amherst, Nova Scotia

Instruments
Fiddle, mandolin, guitar, bass, vocals

> "You can just bring out your guitar, start singing and jam along."

living down there. That's where all my heroes were, and that's where I could experience what the music scene was all about. First I went to New England, where a musician friend, Roger Williams, invited me to stay at his house. He now works with me on a lot of my recordings.

I played in Vermont, North Carolina, Florida and Europe in the first year. Eventually I got to Nashville, and although I was offered some work, I couldn't take it because I didn't have my work papers. So I moved back to the Maritimes in 1990 and started my own bluegrass band, Acoustic Horizon. In 1991, I found out that they had picked my name in a lottery for permanent residency in the States. By then I was already home and playing with my own band, doing some sessions and working steadily, so I decided to stay here.

At that point I also toured with some American groups, including Michelle Shocked. Her *Arkansas Traveler* album was based on traditional fiddle tunes, to which she wrote new lyrics. She wanted a fiddle player, so I toured with her in Canada and Australia. Then we did an American tour, which ended up at Carnegie Hall in November 1993. The Band, from Woodstock, New York, was on this tour. It was quite an experience playing with Levon Helm, Garth Hudson and Rick Danko.

I love bluegrass because the musicians and fans feel close to you. It's acoustic music; you don't need any electricity. You can just bring out your guitar, start singing, and jam along. It's user-friendly. Bluegrass music has roots in Irish and Scottish fiddle tunes and in the mountain music of Kentucky. I guess that's how it caught on here, because we're fiddle fanatics.

discography

- **Common Denominator**/Acoustic Horizon Music, 1991
- **Back Against the Wind**/Acoustic Horizon Music, 1992
- **Maritime Fiddle Session**/Acoustic Horizon Music, 1993
- **A Decade Later (River of No Return)**/Acoustic Horizon Music, 1994
- **River of No Return** (re-release)/Strictly Country Records, 1996

The bluegrass sound is mainly the five-string banjo played three-fingered style, with the mandolin doing a back beat representing a drum. There's a lot of fiddle-playing in there as well. That's the focus of the music, with three-part, and sometimes four-part, harmony. Now bluegrass styles have crossed into the country sound. Many fiddle players who played bluegrass are doing session work in Nashville today.

I've always liked the speed, I'm known as a fast player. I love the acoustic sound and making the harmonies blend. Lately I've been playing a lot of swing music. The old swing was all acoustic. Stéfane Grappelli and the Quintette du Hot Club de France, that's the type of swing I really like. A lot of bluegrass came from the improvisational licks of swing music and jazz, and some of the chord changes are similar. Once in a while I go to Moncton and sit in with the "Jazz Crew" over at the Cosmos Club.

I'm a strong Maritimer, a strong Canadian, but at the same time I want to improve my playing. Bluegrass music is American music. I went to the States to get a good grasp of it, and now I've added to it what we have here — the strong melodic sense and danceable rhythms of fiddle music. Everything I play still has a bluegrass orientation. I can only play like me, and my playing is full of different styles.

I wanted to be where I grew up, home. When I was living in the States, I didn't feel at home. I like the water. I should be near the ocean, I think.

FAN fare

Management
Ray Legere,
46 Albion Street,
Amherst, NS,
B4H 2V5;
(902) 667-4460 (phone);
(902) 661-4460 (fax)
rayleger@atcon.com (e-mail)

Great Sounds

Playing Carnegie Hall was the thrill of a lifetime, knowing that all the greatest performers in the world have stood on that stage. The soundcheck was the best experience for me because I could just play my fiddle acoustically without being plugged in. You could feel the resonance of the room.

Ashley MacIsaac

Ashley MacIsaac is a fiddling phenomenon the likes of which has never been seen before in Canada. Sometimes decried as a heretic by fiddle purists, MacIsaac has methodically set about recasting Cape Breton's musical tradition. He and his band, the Kitchen Devils, have broken new ground for a whole generation of young Maritime musicians who want to express world-music influences through their own strong musical traditions. His debut album certainly includes urban dance anthems and jig-rock salvos, but there are still down-home standards in abundance. MacIsaac has performed with many international stars, but it is his own musical projects that excite him the most.

"The most talented fiddler I've ever seen. Absolutely amazing."
— *Billboard Magazine*

The Mad Step-dancing Fiddle Player

My mom is French, or half French. Her mom was a Leblanc, and her father was a MacNeil. My dad is half Macdonald and half MacIsaac. So I'm three-quarters Scottish with a little Leblanc in there. There's a direct musical line through both sides of the family right back. My father's family were pipers, and his father played the fiddle. His mom, uncles, brothers all played pipes and other instruments. My mom's side were the dancers. A lot of good step-dancers were MacNeils.

Growing up, it was basically fiddle music. I watched a few video music shows and *Good Rockin' Tonight*, but I wasn't much into pop music. Until I was about seventeen, everything that I thought about music was in the fiddle sense. It could've been Gaelic singing or bagpiping, but the majority of it was just straight-ahead Cape Breton fiddle music. Howie MacDonald was a big influence, and Buddy MacMaster was the biggest influence.

I took lessons from a fellow by the name Stan Chapman, who also taught Natalie MacMaster. Stan is the man responsible for the uprising of fiddle among young people.

Now, I'm the link between Celtic music and modern music. Celtic music has 1600 years of oppression. Celtic musicians have always been looking for a place. When they get connected with their sense of home, they are pretty proud of it, almost arrogant because they're so happy about it.

My gig is trying to link what I do to other people. I strive to keep my gigs totally spontaneous. There is always a sense of not knowing exactly what is going to take place in my gig, or what I am going to say next. When I play a strictly traditional gig, I just sit down and play the best I can. But if I'm performing for big venues, shock value and the whole element of surprise come into it. I like to present myself in different lights, whether it be hanging out on the QE II in my tux or being on Hastings Street in Vancouver with all the heroin addicts.

opening notes

Date of birth
February 24, 1975

Place of birth
Antigonish, Nova Scotia

Heritage
Scottish

Language
English

Current residence
Creignish, Cape Breton (NS)

Instrument
Fiddle

> "I am a capitalist fiddler and completely proud of it."

I live in the moment. I have to. I have a devil-may-care attitude that works in what I am doing and in my business — the business of being the mad, step-dancing fiddle player who likes to hang out on the *QE II*. I want to continue with what I am doing. I'm content where I am at this point. I'm enjoying it. I'm riding the wave and I don't know when it will stop.

I am working on a new album with the working title *Ashley MacIsaac Goes Disco 1997: Just Me and a Bunch of Fruits*. It will be quite funny. I have this wonderful picture that someone took of me with all these plastic apples and oranges and bananas. The actual record I am doing is a club record, a dance record, all kinds of hip ideas for just bouncing your baby to.

I believe in industry, because I believe in people being content with their employment. The entertainment industry is the hardest and most fickle one to be involved in. This industry is very emotional. It's all about feelings and people going out and exposing their souls to other people for entertainment purposes. People either want to be an entertainer themselves or they appreciate what a musician is doing because they know they would never do it. But musicians are just people. We all wipe our arse the same way.

I am a fiddler at heart, but I've also had a drive my whole life to make money. I am a capitalist fiddler and completely proud of it. I know that what I'm doing is a very hard way to make money. I'm living a very intense life. It's wonderful, but I would be just as happy sitting home, eating lobsters in Cape Breton, if I didn't have to worry about paying my phone bill. Now I'm finally at the point of realizing my dream of building a house in Cape Breton. I'm

disco**graphy**

- **Close to the Floor**/independent, 1992
- **A Cape Breton Christmas**/independent, 1993
- **Close to the Floor** (re-release)/Ancient Music/A&M, 1995
- **Hi, How Are You Today?**/Ancient Music/A&M, 1995
- **Fine, Thank You Very Much (A Traditional Album)**/Ancient Music/A&M, 1996

sure I'll continue to work, but I have said no to things already because I am content with where I am.

The economy of the Maritimes has always made it necessary for people to leave. They felt they couldn't be self-sufficient and enjoy their lifestyle, that they had to find something somewhere else. Most people who go away would like to come back. But most people who are successful are happy with their position in life wherever they are. In Cape Breton, saying, "Hi, How Are You Today?" gives you an instant connection with people, no matter who they are. Having that simple means to connect has given me the ability to come off in most situations as just being an okay guy, one who has a lot of things in his head, which on the occasion can make him a little bit warped.

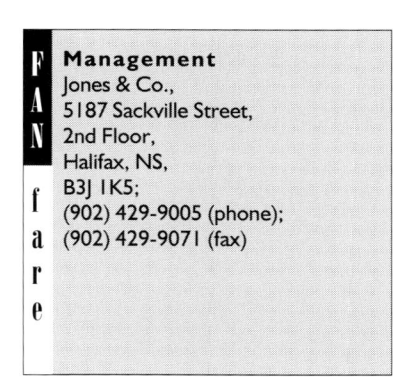

FAN fare

Management
Jones & Co.,
5187 Sackville Street,
2nd Floor,
Halifax, NS,
B3J 1K5;
(902) 429-9005 (phone);
(902) 429-9071 (fax)

The Devil in the Kitchen

I am very connected with air karma, very connected with what is happening around me and what is happening in the world. As a result I've had experiences that just seem way too uncanny. It's like people in San Francisco writing songs about earthquakes just before they took place.

For example, for a whole year before I got asked to go to New York City I went to Halifax to buy *The Village Voice*. Then, out of the blue I was invited to New York to play music. I had known the whole vibe for a year beforehand. I was very open-minded about the city and had lots of fun. Then about two months into it, my dad visited me. We were staying in this house that had had strong spiritual stuff happening in it for the past 150 years. It was a corner brownstone in the East Village and had been owned by the mayor in the 1860s or 1870s. My dad was in a room where there was a *Sunday New York Times*, which weighs about six pounds, sitting on the floor. The newspaper levitated three or four feet off the floor in front of him. When I came back that night, the same thing happened in front of the two of us.

There's lots of spiritual, emotional writing sitting in my black box of notes from the last three years of experiences. I've learned that the most evil you assume could possibly take place still has a sense of uncanny niceness to it and that there is a fine border between it all. The devil's in the kitchen.

Dave MacIsaac

When Halifax string-wizard Dave MacIsaac took away three ECMAs in Charlottetown in 1996 for his recording *Nimble Fingers*, he was shocked, but no one else active in the region's industry was. They all know him as one of the best traditional instrumentalists the Maritimes has ever produced. Dave is also a walking encyclopedia of musical information. And it would be difficult to find a Celtic album recorded in Nova Scotia that doesn't have his name in its credits. Dave grew up listening to Cape Breton fiddle music alongside rock 'n' roll, blues, country and jazz, all of which have influenced his playing. Dave also accompanies and tours with Natalie MacMaster.

Mr. Nimble Fingers

My parents were Gaelic speakers from Cape Breton Island. Dad played the fiddle and was a Gaelic singer, and I guess that's how I get the music. I know a couple of bad words in Gaelic, but that's about all. My grandfather was Sandy Angus MacDonald from Lake Ainslie in Cape Breton, and he played a bit of the fiddle, too. I started playing it when I was about five or six, but took up the guitar after I saw the Beatles on *The Ed Sullivan Show*. The guitar took over for a few years, but I picked up the fiddle again when I was fifteen.

There were always fiddle records around our house, old 78s. I can remember buying them for seventy-five cents each when I was five years old. I bought records by Angus Chisholm, Winston Scotty Fitzgerald, all the great Cape Breton fiddlers, and listened to guitarists like Estwood Davison, who accompanied Scotty. The first electric guitarists I heard were the 1950s rock 'n' rollers — Chuck Berry and James Burton, who played with Ricky Nelson —and country people like Don Rich, Buck Owens, Roy Nichols and Merle Haggard. I always liked hot guitar players, including the English ones like Jeff Beck and Eric Clapton.

My first performance was with my father, Alex Dan. I've been playing professionally for about twenty-three years. Guitar and fiddle are my main instruments, and I also play dobro and mandolin. I've sung backup the odd time, but primarily I'm an instrumentalist. I've worked on the road with people like John Allan Cameron and Natalie MacMaster and recorded as a sideman to musicians such as Natalie MacMaster, Tracey Dares, Jerry Holland, Carl MacKenzie, Buddy MacMaster and the Rankin Family. One of the highlights of my career was sharing the bill and stage with Junior Brown for the "Guitar Wizards" show at Wolftrap, Virginia in 1994. It was a thrill to be on the stage with one of my heroes.

opening notes

Date of birth
February 5, 1955

Place of birth
Halifax, Nova Scotia

Heritage
Scottish

Language
English

Current residence
Halifax, Nova Scotia

Instruments
Acoustic & electric guitars, violin, mandolin, bottleneck dobro, tenor banjo, bass

> "There's always another tune to be learned."

I still live in Halifax where I was born, but when I was playing full time with John Allan between about 1977 and 1982 I spent a lot of time working out of Toronto. John Allan and his wife Angela were good enough to let me crash at their place. Being a professional musician is like being in the circus.

For a musician, the motivation has to be the love of the music, of hearing other people play and seeing the smile on somebody's face when they hear you play. That's what makes it all worthwhile. There's always another tune to be learned. You have to build up your own repertoire. I like digging up old Celtic music, collecting books from around the world and trading tapes with people from all over the place. I've got tapes of fiddle music from Cape Breton from 1929 right up to the present. I enjoy playing tunes that other people don't play. Recently, I've been doing the music for the "Mystery Project," a series of CBC radio dramas with Scott Macmillan. I'm always lining up music for recording projects. If I'm going through an old book, I might put a mark by a tune to learn.

The roots of East Coast music run very deep. Celtic music goes back to people's parents, grandparents, and great-grandparents, generations of playing music, fiddling, singing and step-dancing. The music is in my family and several others, people like the Rankins, the Barra MacNeils, and, of course, Natalie MacMaster's family. A lot of good blues and rhythm and blues are being played around here, too, by people like Dutch Mason, Matt Minglewood and Joe Murphy.

The East Coast Music Awards have certainly helped take our music to a national audience and into the United States. People from *Rolling Stone* and other major magazines were at the Awards, checking out the scene in the Maritimes. I think they were impressed. The showcases were all great.

discography

- **Celtic Music of Cape Breton, Volume I**/UCCB Press, 1984
- **Celtic Guitar**/independent, 1986
- **Guitar Souls, Live** (with Scott Macmillan)/Atlantica, 1993
- **Nimble Fingers**/Pickin' Productions, 1995

A Crashing Tune

In 1980 a bunch of us — John Allan Cameron, Stan Rogers, Barry Shears, Father George MacInnis, and Jennifer Whalen (now Jennifer Quinn) — were performing over in Scotland. There was this big do, a big supper for all these highfalutin' lairds and ladies, and we were the entertainers. The back legs of my chair were a little too close to the edge of the stage, and I leaned back and went flying. One second I was there and the next I wasn't. This was in the opening number of John Allan's tune. He heard all this banging and crashing and said, "What the hell's going on back there?"

Somehow I got back up on the stage and grabbed my fiddle. I was kind of wobbly, and instead of going back and forth with the bow, I was going in the wrong direction, from the bridge to the end of the fingerboard, I was so rattled. It took me a little while to get the bow motion going again. I'm just lucky I didn't break my neck.

Every type of music you play helps you play all the other types better. You get around your instrument in ways that you wouldn't ordinarily, different scales, different grooves. For example, I play blues fiddle with the bow or with the fingers in a way that I wouldn't play Celtic music. It all helps you become more proficient on your instrument.

My advice is don't be closed-minded about other types of music; just listen to everything, keep your ears open and keep practicing. And play in tune, tune your instrument! There are only two types of music: there's well played and there is not-so-well played.

FANfare

Management
Pickin' Productions,
P.O. Box 46043,
Novalea RPO,
Halifax, NS,
B3K 5V8;
(902) 454-5555 (phone);
(902) 454-9295 (fax)

Natalie MacMaster

Cape Breton fiddler Natalie MacMaster is one of the most celebrated fiddle players ever to grace a stage. She has toured North America and as far away as New Zealand. On stage she seems to dance the night away as her entire body moves to the music.

Brought up steeped in the heritage of her Scottish ancestors, Natalie took lessons from Stan Chapman of Antigonish. She was encouraged by her father and influenced by her uncle, Buddy MacMaster, recognized as one of the undisputed masters of the Cape Breton fiddle.

Natalie's first three recordings have garnered major nominations and awards from the East Coast Music Association. In 1995, she was nominated as Entertainer of the Year. She signed with a major label for her fourth recording, *No Boundaries*.

The Dancing Fiddler

I don't know too many fiddlers who don't know how to step-dance. It's not that the fiddle goes hand in hand with dancing, but in Cape Breton, everyone can step-dance. That's the truth, pretty near. They can do the hop step, the basic step, and that will get them through the square set. I come from a long line of musicians, singers and dancers on both sides. My father's parents were very musical. His father played the fiddle, and his aunts played tunes on the piano and the fiddle. My aunts are all piano players, singers and step-dancers. Buddy MacMaster, the fiddler, is my uncle. My mother's mother was also a very musical lady. She danced, and she taught all her children to dance. She jigged the tunes with her mouth. She probably enjoyed music as much as anyone I ever met in my life. My mom was quite a well known step-dancer in her day. Minnie Beaton is her maiden name.

She taught me to step-dance when I was five. I also competed in Highland dancing for twelve years, which is totally different from step-dancing. It's more competitive. It's its own thing entirely. I first picked up the fiddle when I was nine and a half. My dad taught me for the first six months, then I took fiddle lessons from Stan Chapman for three years. As far as combining dancing and fiddling, that happened only about three or four years ago. It came about through this group of seven young artists who played piano and fiddle and who step-danced. We decided at the end of one of our shows that we would all step-dance and play the fiddle at the same time. We had heard that Jerry Holland did it when he was a kid. Everybody thought it was great.

The first time I tried dancing and playing at the same time, I couldn't do it. The second time I tried it, just in the kitchen, I got a step or two out. Then I tried it again and got a few more steps out, but the bow was just bouncing up and down. I wasn't even playing a tune. It sounded as if I was dancing with my fiddle. I

opening notes

Date of birth
June 13, 1972

Place of birth
Antigonish, Nova Scotia

Heritage
Scottish

Language
English

Current residence
Troy, Cape Breton (NS)

Instruments
Fiddle, piano

> "The culture comes across in our music."

knew then that I had to figure something out. So I practised a lot and concentrated on my playing, on making sure my bow stayed where it was supposed to be. I just kept my feet going. If they messed up, it didn't matter. It looked like a step! Over time I've also picked up some different steps from other places and people. Now I have a combination, and anything goes. It's all my own. It's got some Irish, some Appalachian clogging, and some moonwalk too! Some of the old steps may get lost. That's inevitable. No matter where you live in the world, something is going to get lost. Somebody is going to forget a step, and it will never be remembered. We're going to run out of steps if we don't create new ones. Or we can take elements of the old steps and make new ones. My mother has done that. She has made up her own steps. She always told me I was a different step-dancer. I always danced on my toes, whereas everybody else uses their heels when they shuffle. I've always had a different flare. Now I'm just doing steps from different cultures.

I've toured with the Chieftains. I opened for Carlos Santana once in front of 100,000 people. That was really cool. It was also kind of weird. "Sure, I'll do it," I thought, "but what the heck are they thinking? I'm a fiddler." But anything goes nowadays. It's great. All different types of music are accepted and nothing is seen as uncool. I was born at a good time. All the great performers before me gave people a good taste of what the music is down here. I guess people just liked the trueness and the coming-from-the-heart sound we have here. The culture comes across in our music.

I want to spread the music around. I want to be able to play all across Canada, in the States, the U.K., and in Europe, wherever it will take me. I know there are markets for this music out there. I

discography

- **Four to the Floor**/independent, 1989
- **Road to the Isle**/independent, 1991
- **Fit as a Fiddle**/independent, 1993
- **No Boundaries**/Warner Music Canada, 1996

want to experience them. I want to see how far can I take this in Denmark or Oklahoma. It's an adventure.

I want to make a good go of it, but I don't like being away for any longer than a month. And if I am away for that long, I have to get home for a week in between. I'm driven, but I'm not overpoweringly. I love coming home, and I love the elements of home. I love the thoughts of getting married and having kids and someday living in a nice house and being happy in a little community. Then there's the opposite of all that, the career woman, the one travelling all over the world, signing autographs. I'm driven with my career, but not to the point that it would take away from my home life. Cape Breton will always be home.

I have lots of ideas. I am a huge lover of all different music styles and I love playing different things. Any time I hear a new beat or a new sound or a new voice or a new language, I ask myself how I can incorporate it with my fiddle tunes. It's all I think of. Anything could happen.

FAN fare

Management
André Bourgeois,
Ground Swell Production,
P.O. Box 245, Central Station,
Halifax, NS,
B3J 2N7;
(902) 492-0744 (phone);
(902) 492-0259 (fax)

A High Kick

I was performing in Kentucky and was about to do this dance step I call my Bell Click Step. It's when you click your heels in the air like on the cover of my *Fit as a Fiddle* album. The crowd was all standing around me and clapping. I went to do the step, but when I swung my foot up, I caught my heel on a crack in the stage. I fell right fair and square on my butt. The audience gasped, but I stood up and said, "That's all part of my show, folks." And then I limped off the stage.

Scott Macmillan

Scott Macmillan's musical résumé gives an indication of the incredible talent of this Halifax native. He has his finger in so many different musical pies — blues, jazz, folk, traditional and classical — and he has recorded with, or arranged and produced for, the who's who of East Coast music. He is an associate composer with the Canadian Music Centre and Host Conductor of the Mostly Maritime Pops Series for Symphony Nova Scotia. His composition "Celtic Mass for the Sea," with a libretto by his wife and musical collaborator Jennyfer Brickenden, has garnered critical acclaim from coast to coast. It has been described as a "thrilling, striking and imagined work" which "delves into the soul and heritage" of seafaring peoples.

MORROW SCOT-BROWN

An Expression of Heart and Soul

My father's family is from Charlottetown. The Macmillans are Barra Macmillans, from the Isle of Barra. My mother's family was originally from Belfast, Prince Edward Island. Mother was a MacLeod. The Irish in me comes from my grandmother on my father's side, May Carroll Macmillan. She played the violin and the piano by ear. She played the popular music of the time at house parties, and was a regular poetry contributor to the Charlottetown Guardian.

I got interested in music on my own time. When I was in Grade Six my brother, Mark, brought the first of many guitars into our house and I started learning by playing along with records or with songs on the radio. I was pretty shy, but after a couple of years I realized I could play what they were playing on the records, and I thought, "Hey, I could do that. Maybe I'm pretty good at this thing and I don't even know it."

In Grade Nine I got a little rock 'n' roll band together with friends on the block. The first time we performed I was so nervous that although the rest of the band stood to play, I played sitting down. In high school, I met Dave MacIsaac and got into the blues. Eric Clapton, B.B. King and Buddy Guy were important influences. As well, at this time, Dave introduced me to Cape Breton music.

I took a BA in mathematics. In my third year of university, I took an elective classical-guitar course. It was a big eye-opener for me. All of a sudden I realized that the guitar could be quite difficult to play. Up to that point I just learned things that came naturally, but, taking classical guitar, I began to realize the complexity of the instrument. After I graduated I spent a year on a rock 'n' roll road trip, playing in a band called Rock Talk. We put a lot of work into getting the band to sound good, but after a while we decided to do original songs. That's when my desire to go back to school started. I had many years of playing and working out music by ear. When I brought my songs to the band, I had difficulty showing them what

opening notes

Date of birth
April 25, 1955

Place of birth
Halifax, Nova Scotia

Current residence
Halifax, Nova Scotia

Instruments
Conductor/composer/arranger, guitar, piano

> "Music is an expression of the heart and soul."

I wanted to do. It became clear to me that I needed a deeper understanding of how to realize my own musical ideas.

I took classical guitar at the Dalhousie music department for a year and then I went to Humber College in Toronto. Before I went to Humber, I had to decide whether to concentrate on being an instrumentalist or a composer/arranger. My wife, Jennyfer, helped me through this. I finally decided to let the guitar take care of itself and to concentrate on the writing. That decision was important because it facilitated all the other decisions I made down the line.

I think the single most important influence on my music was the experience of starting off with the blues. It has taught me the emotional side of music, how it can reach deep down into the soul. As well, on a more technical level, playing the blues showed me how to listen and how to carry on a musical dialogue with the other members of the band. This training has paid off in all the different styles of music that I play. I can truthfully say that I've put in long hard hours at developing my writing and performing skills, to the point that waking up at 5 AM is regular fare for me; the phone tends to be quiet at that time of day. So, if I was to label myself I would say I'm a "hard worker who plays the blues."

I see music as an expression of the heart and soul. I enjoy all kinds of music; I have a desire to understand it and to be an active part of it. It can give healing and joy to all people. It is a language that transcends the spoken word.

select discography

- **Guitar Souls, Live** (co-producer, composer & performer)/Atlantica, 1993
- **Celtic Mass for the Sea** (composer & arranger)/Marquis Classics, 1994
- **The Rankin Family: Endless Seasons** (preproduction)/EMI Music Canada, 1995
- **The Rankin Family; Collection** (co-location producer for one song)/EMI Music Canada, 1996
- **Scott Macmillan Presents the "Minnie Sessions Volume 1"** (composer, arranger, co-producer & performer)/Tamarac Records, 1996
- **Rita MacNeil; Joyful Sounds: A Seasonal Collection** (co-producer & arranger for 2 songs)/EMI Music Canada, 1996
- *Puirt a Baroque*; **Bach Meets Cape Breton** (co-arranger & performer, composer for 2 songs)/Marquis Classics, 1996

I work with a multitude of diverse styles of music found here in Nova Scotia. Writing an ever-increasing number of arrangements for classical musicians, I've come to see myself as a link between the classical and non-classical communities. Maintaining the integrity of each musical expression when combining them creates a rich and meaningful example of community development for both the performers and the audience.

"Celtic Mass for the Sea" was written for a mixed choir, a Celtic ensemble and string orchestra or quartet. It is based on the Celtic Prayers, which go back as far as the fourth or fifth century and were translated into English in the early twentieth century. Jennyfer Brickenden was the librettist, and I wrote the music. I tip my hat to the CBC. They commissioned us to compose a piece for the creatures of the sea. We wanted it to have a Celtic flavour — hence the title. It was a nice opportunity to take our own environmental concerns and work them into the piece and do it by using an ancient text. The audience was overwhelmed. They just loved it. It has done phenomenally well for a classical recording. It has touched a lot of people, I think, because the text is so old and the music has such strong rooting in traditional background. It touches people on an intuitive level and becomes a deep part of their lives. It's exciting and humbling at the same time to know that your music is making that impact on people's lives.

> **FAN fare**
>
> **Management/bookings**
> Marilyn Gilbert Artists Management,
> 18 Bracondale Hill Road,
> Toronto, ON,
> M6G 3P4;
> (416) 657-8224 (phone);
> (416) 657-8228 (fax)
>
> **Fan mail**
> Scott Macmillan,
> 5543 Sebastian Place,
> Halifax, NS,
> B3K 2K5;
> (902) 455-6325 (phone);
> (902) 453-9344 (fax);
> scojen@auracom.com (e-mail)

A Confusion of Saints

We were doing *Evita* at the Neptune Theatre in Halifax. I was playing guitar. Zappa Costa was playing a lead part. At one point he is supposed to announce from offstage that another member of the cast will sing a song about an earthquake in San Juan, Argentina. It is part of the story of the show. But Zappa Costa made a mistake. Out of his mouth came "St. John's" and then "Newfoundland." The entire company of about twenty actors and the band of five were pissing themselves laughing. Right after the song, there was a dramatic scene in which one of the actors had a gun. Breaking character and bending over laughing in that scene was not such a good idea, but the actors couldn't hold it. Being in the pit, I couldn't see the audience, but I could see everything else and what a scene that was.

Rita MacNeil

Over the past twenty years, Rita MacNeil has delivered twelve albums that have earned her awards, accolades and the respect of the music industry. Her platinum and double platinum sales in Canada and abroad are testimony to her continuing popularity as a performer. Rita is the recipient of three Juno Awards, four Canadian Country Music Awards, five honorary doctorates, seven East Coast Music Awards, and in 1992 she accepted the Order of Canada. In addition to a busy touring schedule, Rita is also the host of the top-rated CBC television show, Rita & Friends, and is the owner of Rita's Tea Room, located in Big Pond, Cape Breton.

IVAN OTIS

A Belief in Music

I'm the middle child of eight. My family called Big Pond, in Cape Breton, home. It's a small town of 200, with a lot of MacNeils. I spent a lot of time outdoors as a child, and I always marvelled at the lake and the beauty.

I listened to the radio every chance I got. It didn't matter what was playing — I'd listen to everything from Celtic to rock to Hawaiian music. I sang along to all the songs. As a teenager, I could hardly wait to be able to come home from school and put the radio on. My mother loved to hear me sing. She knew I was too shy to sing for anyone else. She believed in my singing and so wanted me to be able to one day perform, because she knew that's what I loved. When I moved away from home, she would phone up to see how things were going. She knew that I would always be out there pursuing the career from one stage to another. I hoped she would be able to see me one day, but she passed away before things started to happen for me. That was a bit of a rough time. I wrote the song "Reason to Believe" in 1988 about it, and that brought her closer again.

When I was seventeen, I left home for Toronto to pursue my music. I had some really hard times for many years. A lot of songs came out of those hard times and you learn a lot about yourself. In the late 1970s, I moved back to Cape Breton for good. That's when my career took a better direction. The writing seemed to open up more and I was re-introduced to my roots. It was great because I connected with musicians from home and that brought everything into focus. I had lots of good times in the clubs on the East Coast, Cape Breton in particular. Music is so appreciated and loved there. I can remember getting ready to go to gigs and it was always a joyous event, it seemed to bring people so close.

I have a strong sense of music. I can hear melodies and instrumental parts even though I don't know how to write down or play what I hear. When I'm lost for an idea, I go inside myself. It works

opening notes

Date of birth
May 28

Place of birth
Big Pond, Cape Breton (NS)

Language
English

Current residence
Big Pond, Cape Breton (NS)

Instrument
Vocals

> "When I'm lost for an idea, I go inside myself."

every time. The melodies are very clear and strong. The words usually come fairly easily. It's almost as though they're on a string. Sometimes I think there's nothing left to draw on, but, without fail, inspiration finds me. My songs are not just about me, they're about everybody.

My most recent album, Porch Songs, has more vocal and less production. The producer, Don Potter, is a very sensitive and caring man, and he was always able to hear me sing a song and then get to the right sound. We wanted to break things down to a more simple and direct style because of the songs. They seemed to dictate that. They're reflective, so we wanted to keep the production a little more in the background.

My favourite place is Cape Breton Island. It's a place of extraordinary beauty. I know when the sun goes down this is where I will leave my soul. It's a place I keep coming back to. When I'm away from here, I tend to get misty-eyed and I write lines like these: "As far as the eyes can see these fields are green now. And the blue horizon takes my breath away. In the rolling hills, my life I will remember. Oh the endless hours and carefree days." I realize how truly lucky I am. I get to live here, and I have the opportunity to tour the rest of the world. I have this great urge to encourage everyone to visit and see what I feel and tell through my songs. The passion I feel for this place I call home.

When I started to get acceptance and recognition for my music, it was wonderful. I'd always wanted to sing and I had an inner need to express myself. That's why I became a musician. Although I'm quite shy, my belief in my music has helped me persevere and

select discography

- **Born A Woman**/independent, 1975
- **Flying On Your Own**/Lupins/Virgin-A&M, 1987
- **Reason To Believe**/Lupins/Virgin-A&M, 1988
- **Volume One (Songs from The Collection)**/Lupins/Virgin-A&M, 1994
- **Porch Songs**/EMI Music Canada, 1995
- **Joyful Sounds: A Seasonal Collection** (re-release)/EMI Music Canada, 1996

face the stage. My dream was always to be a singer. Never in my wildest dreams did I think it would happen.

While concert tours are a big part of my life and I love the time I spend on the road, I'm also glad that I'm able to fit in the television show. I don't know how, but I'm doing it! It's turning out to be a wonderful experience. The guest lists have been very diverse. I'm getting to meet performers I've loved and admired for years, and others whose work I didn't know.

I think East Coast music is being embraced now, due to the fact that it has received the exposure and the attention. It's been brought into the forefront, into the mainstream of the musical world, and it has proven to have a wide appeal. Being from the East Coast is wonderful, and being a musician from this part is even better, as the wealth of music here certainly keeps your head turning. Music has been a part of our culture for so long. There are other parts of Canada that can say the same thing, in many respects, but the history of hardships associated with the East Coast, especially Cape Breton, has given a strength to its people and an appreciation for music, that is evident.

FAN fare

Management
Lupins Productions,
P.O. Box 183,
Sydney, NS,
B1P 6H1;
(902) 539-8874 (phone);
(902) 562-7012 (fax);
lupins@fox.nstn.ca (e-mail)

Website
http://www.ritamacneil.com/tea

And the next speaker is ...

Once, I was asked to perform at Humber College in Toronto. When I got there, I discovered that, although I knew I was a singer, they thought I was a speaker, and they had a room full of people waiting to hear me speak. I had no choice but to perform. It was sort of like a speech opera. I have no idea what I said, but from that day on I made sure everyone knew exactly what I do — sing!

Theresa Malenfant

Winner of the 1995 East Coast Music Award for Female Artist of the Year, Theresa Malenfant sings with deep conviction and plenty of soul. She made her stage debut as a teenager when Dutch Mason invited her out of the audience to jam with his band. In 1979 she went on to form her own group, the Black 'n Blues Band, and has since become well known in clubs and jazz festivals across Canada. Her third album, *Eye of the Hurricane*, capitalizes on her innate blues ability and takes her into related areas, including rhythm and blues.

A Blues Singer Amidst Bagpipes and Fiddles

I started singing when I was about five, maybe even younger. I fell right in love with singing. In Grade One, I was asked what I wanted to be when I grew up. All the girls in the class said nurses, teachers, hairdressers, and the boys said firemen, policemen and stuff. I said I wanted to be Julie Andrews or Doris Day or Patti Page.

My mother's younger sister, Carolyn, who is just nine years older than me, spent most of her teenage years in our house. I got to listen to a lot of music through her — all the stuff coming out in the 1960s, like Stevie Wonder, the Supremes and Isaac Hayes. When Carolyn married my uncle Bill, who is Black, I finally got a chance to hear what I am doing now. Bill was right into it. He loved Junior Walker and the All Stars, and the old stuff that I'm just freaked out about now, and Al Green, who is my favourite male vocalist of all time. That's where I first heard soul and R&B. I grew up listening to this stuff.

When I hit ten, I lost myself in singing. I spent hours and hours singing. You talk about kids going out and playing sports and tag and stuff. Not me. I was in my room with my record player, singing. When I was twelve my mother bought me three Janis Joplin albums for Christmas. I fell in love with her singing.

As I got a little older I started to do a lot of drugs. Before that I probably had the highest grades in my class. Soon my grades started to go down and I had no interest in school. I thought I didn't need to learn anything. But I never lost my interest in music. I still wanted to be a singer. Now I wish I'd stayed in school and got my education. I am so in awe of people with an education. At nineteen I quit taking drugs, and to this day I have not done drugs. I don't smoke or drink much either. I have the fear of God. I am a true believer in the mind and I could feel it going. I wanted to be able to make sense when I spoke, and when people looked at me I wanted them to say,

opening notes

Date of birth
February 27, 1958; Pisces

Place of birth
Dieppe, New Brunswick

Heritage
Acadian, English/Irish

Languages
English, French

Current residence
Halifax, Nova Scotia

Instrument
Vocals

> "In this business, you have to be willing to sacrifice."

"Hey, she's pretty intelligent." I don't think a person who takes drugs can keep it up all their life.

I was eighteen the first time I saw blues music live: Dutch Mason was playing in my home town. He always liked to invite people up.

"Why don't you get up?" my friends were saying.

"I don't know how to sing that kind of music, " I said.

"You can do it. Do that Janis Joplin song you know."

I knew two verses of a song of hers called "Turtle Blues." And of course I had a few drinks in me. I got up and I sang with Dutchie Mason. I sang "Turtle Blues." I was hooked. Dutchie thought I was really good and asked me to come back that night. I did and I sang the same song. I don't think I was singing it correctly. It was more of a screamer. But people really liked how I did it.

I got my start singing in a gay bar in the city of Moncton. I was a regular, I was there every night of the week. I sang there with a few other guys. It was just fun. We did blues and stuff.

I'm a blues singer in a place where everyone thinks the only kind of music is bagpipes and fiddles. For some reason the older people have really taken a liking to me. They say I'm going to be the next Rita MacNeil. I don't mind that they are the older crowd because they are so dedicated. I am still doing quite well, because I'm one of the few female blues singers in Atlantic Canada. I don't have a lot of competition, and there are a lot of blues fans. The top blues singer, Dutch Mason, comes from Atlantic Canada.

My album, *Eye of the Hurricane*, featured fourteen artists from Atlantic Canada and eleven original songs written by Atlantic Canadians. It was my dream to put out a piece to help all the artists. It was a real East Coast collaborative effort.

discography

- **Turtle Blues**/independent, 1990
- **Your Good Thing**/independent, 1992
- **Eye of the Hurricane**/independent, 1994
- **Little Girl Blue**/independent, 1997 release

I've made a lot of friends. We have a tight-knit little blues community. And we have survived. Because we are from Atlantic Canada, we have always looked out for ourselves. We are not back-stabbers; we try to help each other. If we find a gig that's not our thing, we will lead it to someone else. We have our ups and downs, and we have our words. Everyone gets pretty cranky on the road. But we are all musicians, and we know what it's like. We've been through it all. You either throw in the towel or get along. I try to get along. In this business, you have to be willing to sacrifice. If you're willing to sacrifice and you have it in you, then you should follow your dream. If you don't, you're always going to wonder if you could have done it.

I've already achieved success. I'm a singer. That's all I wanted. I've never wanted to win awards although I'm not going to refuse them. I wanted to get up and sing and have people want to listen to me. But if no one had wanted to listen to me, I'd have sung in the shower. I would have been thirty-eight years old and still in my bedroom with my CD player.

I'm not a songwriter. I can't do it. People tell me I can, but I just can't find the words. I have a head full of so many songs that I've been singing for so many years that, every time I think about a song, all the old songs come back. I'd be charged with plagiarism or something. I know who I am. I'm a singer.

> **FANfare**
>
> **Management**
> TMC Production,
> 6015 Charles Street,
> Halifax, NS,
> B3K 1K9;
> (902) 422-6391 (phone)

Two Big Women

Back in 1990, I was performing at a bar in Cape Bald, New Brunswick, and I was taking a break between sets. This women came up to me. She had tears in her eyes. I thought she was going to tell me that someone had died or something. She walked up to me, grabbed my hand, and looked me in the eyes.

"Oh, I think you're wonderful," she said.

"Thank you," I said.

"I saw your Christmas special."

I realized then that she thought I was Rita MacNeil. I don't sound anything like Rita MacNeil. That's like comparing me to Madonna. We do not do the same type of music. I don't wear the dresses on stage. I don't wear the hat. But we're both big women. Is that where this poor woman's mind is? "Big woman. She must be Rita MacNeil." It has happened so many times to me now that I'm actually getting used to it, and just laugh it off.

Doris Mason

Doris Mason has made entertaining her life's work. An accomplished singer, pianist and songwriter, she has performed a variety of genres, from blues to Scottish and traditional, swing, jazz and pop.

In 1979, she co-founded the popular Mason Chapman Band. For ten years, she was the band leader for the well-known musical comedies *The Rise and Follies of Cape Breton Island* and *Cape Breton Summertime Revue*. Doris has worked on many recording projects, including Rita MacNeil's *Flying on Your Own* recording. Her song "Don't Look Back" was recorded on Theresa Malenfant's most recent recording. Her own debut solo recording *Photograph* is a collection of twelve original songs.

Music in My Blood

I have always been into music: it's in my blood, in my bones. I don't know what I'd do if I didn't do that. My mom loves music. I'm sure when I was in my mom's womb there was music playing all the time. And certainly my dad had a lot to do with that.

When I was young, my grandmother gave us a piano because, with a family of nine, we couldn't really afford it. It was great to have. I couldn't get enough of it. I started playing when I was three, and writing songs when I was five. My dad would teach me little tunes and I'd play them back. My dad played the fiddle, saxophone and a little guitar. He enjoyed playing Don Messer songs, and of course he loved Winston Scotty Fitzgerald. When he was young, he played with Hank Snow. Hank asked him to go on the road but my dad decided to be a family man instead. He loved teaching me. I therefore already had two years of playing under my belt when I started taking lessons from the nuns in primary school. The lessons were pretty basic, and I used to memorize them just like that. I'd pretend I was reading the music when I was basically playing by ear. About three years down the road, the pieces started getting harder. I'd get one of my sisters to play the music for me and then I'd pick it up from there. One day the nun put a brand-new piece of music in front of me and said, "Here. Play that." It was awful. I had to face the music and start looking at the page. Since my lessons were on Mondays, on Sunday nights I'd take all the covers off and sleep with the window open trying to catch a cold so that I didn't have to go to my lesson. But it never occurred to me to quit.

In Grade Six I switched to a new school and a new music teacher. Vesta Mosher asked me where I wanted to start. She put the power in my hands. "Well, I think I'm ready to start at Grade Four of the Royal Conservatory," I said. She was smart to make it an issue of pride: If you think you're at a Grade Four level, you should be accountable for it. That turned me around!

opening notes

Date of birth
September 1, 1959

Place of birth
New Glasgow, Nova Scotia

Heritage
Irish, Scottish, a little Welsh

Language
English

Current residence
Halifax, Nova Scotia

Instruments
Vocals, keyboards

"If it is good music, I am into it."

When I was fourteen, my sister, Clare, and I performed at the Multicultural Festival in Sydney, Cape Breton. We also performed for the Queen here in Halifax, and we went to Ottawa for another Multicultural Festival later that year. Then, the next year, we performed at the Montreal Olympics. When I was fifteen I did the *Who's New* show on the CBC. There I met and worked with the "CBC Mafia" — brilliant musicians in the house band — Skip Beckwith, Donnie Palmer, Tim Cahoon and Paul Mason (no relation).

I moved to Halifax fresh out of high school and started working on the weekends with a band called Natural Affair, replacing Paul Mason. In 1978 I joined a full-time band called Tom Cat. We did a lot of Tom Scott and Average White Band and Tower of Power music and, of course, some disco stuff. At the time I felt like a small fish in a big pond; I was doing a lot of things I'd never done before. I was just shoved out on stage and told to take a solo. Even though I had no jazz training, I was doing a lot of jazzy stuff. I used to lie awake at night with disco tunes going through my head. I got so distraught that I would cry at the drop of a hat. Finally, I was so miserable that I told myself, "If you think you're so good, prove it." I started taking lessons and working on myself and I dispelled the anxiety. I just said I'd do my best and that's all I can do. That was a big lesson for me.

Bette MacDonald, a well-known Cape Breton comedian, and I worked together in the *Cape Breton Revue*, an annual summer music show. After three years she decided to do a one-woman show. I said, "Let's do a two-women show instead. Between us we can't

disco graphy

- **Mason Chapman**/MCR (CBC Maritimes), 1982
- **Rise & Follies**/Cape Breton Music and Theatre Company, 1985
- **The Cape Breton Summertime Revue**/Summertime Productions Society, 1986-1994
- **Photograph**/Atlantica, 1995
- "John Gracie" on **A Gene MacLellan Tribute**/Atlantica, 1995
- **Stan Rogers: An East Coast Tribute (Vols. 1 & 2)** (keyboards)/Atlantica/Duckworth, 1995
- "If You Were Mine" and "You're Beauty" on **Minnie Sessions, Vol. 1** (with Scott Macmillan)/Atlantica, 1996

lose." We thought it would last for something like six weeks. Well, two and a half years later, we were still doing *Beulah Claxton*. The show was incredibly popular and a scream to boot!

Eventually I decided to make an album. I had lots of material. People would often ask me if they could buy anything of mine and I had nothing to give them. So I decided to take the bull by the horns and get in the studio. *Photograph* took seventeen days to record in October 1994. I used seventeen musicians. I told Scott Macmillan, the producer, that I wanted a cello, viola and violin on a tune I wrote for *Beula* called "She Can't Help It." It's a very cathartic song. I wrote the music just after my dad died. It deals with a lot of issues that touch people in different ways. People have come up to me and said, "I was abused as a child and that song really is about me." A lady wrote to say that she has been able to deal with things in her life and she has moved on because of the song. Of course, that brought me to tears; that's why I'm doing what I do. I like to figure out what makes people tick.

I'm proud to be from the East Coast, but I've never been limited by the definition of what music from here is suppose to be. I could be doing this elsewhere. I have been influenced by specific people, but I am also eclectic and like different styles. My mandate is: If it is good music, I'm into it. I write everything, from jazz to Celtic. I will continue to do that until the day I die.

FAN fare

Management
Doris Mason
P.O. Box 903, Central CRO,
Halifax, NS,
B3J 2V9;
(902) 499-7371 (phone);
(902) 445-3311 (fax)

Mistaken Identity

I'm often asked if I'm any relation to Dutchie Mason. One night I was playing piano, and my friend Kenny MacKay came up to play a little saxophone with me. Kenny is a rather large, jolly guy. Anyway this guy came up to me and said, "I love your music, dear. It's really, really great. I especially liked your first album *Strange Brew*." Well, the title of the album is *Special Brew* and it's Dutch Mason's not mine, and for another thing I am a woman. But for some reason when he heard the Mason name, this guy somehow could not tell the difference between me, on keyboards, and Dutchie, a guy who sings the blues and plays the guitar. I guess people get disoriented when they recognize something but they don't know why.

By the way, Dutch introduces me as his wife now. We like to perpetuate the myth.

Dutch Mason

NIGEL MASON

Dutch has lived the blues. His illustrious career spans three decades. His love for the blues started when he first heard B.B. King on the jukebox in his father's restaurant. He played the blues in his home town of Lunenburg before anyone there had heard of the blues. Forty years later, Dutch is still singing the blues. His recent recording *Appearing Nightly* recaptures a time when Dutch was known not only for his trademark vocals, but also for his hot guitar work. The album consists of tracks recorded in 1980, before Dutch was stricken by arthritis and put down his guitar for good. Always ready to share the spotlight and his knowledge, Dutch has assisted countless young musicians.

The Prime Minister of the Blues

I was born at home in Lunenburg, Nova Scotia. Because I weighed only two and a half pounds, my mother and grandmother wrapped me up and put me in cotton batting in an incubator-like thing. I was tenacious from the get-go.

We're German-Dutch. When we moved to Kentville in the Annapolis Valley, I had an accent, so the minute I went to school, everybody started calling me "Dutchie." That's how I got my nickname. My given name is Norman, after my grandfather.

My parents were both professional musicians. My father played stand-up bass and drums, and my mother played piano in the pit for silent movies. She's from Lunenburg and used to go out with Hank Snow. Hank was playing country music in those days. My parents were playing Dixieland music in different bands. So I grew up with Dixieland music.

One day, when I was in my early teens, the drummer in my mother's band got sick, so I filled in. I knew how to keep a beat on the drums because Dad had a set at home. That's how I started playing Dixieland music. When I was growing up, I didn't hear fiddle music that much. Everybody I knew was playing Dixieland music, an altogether different thing. It was dance music, but not old-time dance music. Dixieland was for modern dancing, and everybody jived to it.

In Lunenburg there were no Black people. I'd never seen a Black person until I moved to the Annapolis Valley when I was about ten. In the valley there is a Black community named Gibson Woods. I used to go there and play with all the Black guys. That's how I learned to play guitar when I was about sixteen back in 1955.

When I first started playing, Elvis Presley, Jerry Lee Lewis, and Carl Perkins were popular, and I decided to start a band. I looked something like Jerry Lee Lewis then; everybody did: hair all combed back and the pinstripe suit and the blue suede shoes. Rockabilly

opening notes

Date of birth
February 19, 1938;
Aquarius & Pisces

Place of birth
Lunenburg, Nova Scotia

Heritage
German, Dutch

Language
English

Current residence
Truro, Nova Scotia

Instruments
Vocals, guitar

> "There were a lot of times we didn't work or eat."

songs like "That's All Right, Momma" were our thing. My father used to play stand-up bass with the band, and my mother played with us for a while. I played acoustic guitar, and we had drums and electric guitar. In 1956, we had a fifteen-minute radio show on CKEN in Kentville. Because we couldn't play well enough, my parents would come on the show and we would take requests. That first band was called the Wreckers. After that we formed a real band and called it Dutch Mason and the Esquires. I got listening to the jukebox in my father's restaurant. The sales guy would come in and sell my father 78s but would leave about ten extra records. One was "Sweet Little Angel" by B.B. King. As soon as I heard B.B. King, I knew what I wanted to play. I forgot all about rock 'n' roll and all the rest. I used to have to go to the radio station to get blues records. I was listening to Rufus Thomas, Albert King and James Brown before they made it big.

The blues comes from your heart. You feel that kind of music. I can listen to a fiddle and it's nice, but it doesn't do anything for me. We didn't know anything about blues. We just started playing, and over the years we wove our way into it. We would play blues at dances, and people would leave the floor. The guys in the band would look at me and say, "Geez, we can't keep playing this stuff." "They'll get use to it," I said. And they did. It took about thirty years, but they got used to it.

We had everything in the world going against us. If the band had had a fiddle, we'd have done a hundred percent better. We were all from small towns in Nova Scotia, which was a back step

---

select discography

- **Blue's Ain't Bad**/Wyse Owl Productions, 1976
- **Wish Me Luck**/London Records, 1978
- **Special Brew**/Attic Records, 1980
- **Gimme a Break**/Attic Records, 1982
- **I'm Back**/Stony Plain Records, 1991
- **You Can't Have Everything**/Stony Plain Records, 1992
- **Dutch Mason Appearing Nightly**/Alive Presentations, 1996

for anybody in music then, and we were playing Black people's music from down south. In small towns, people didn't understand what we were doing at all. And neither did we. But we kept on playing. Have you got to suffer to play the blues? Well, we suffered just by playing what we wanted to play. All the guys who played with me were real loyal to it, too. There were a lot of times we didn't work or eat, but we kept playing it anyway. In Nova Scotia nobody played the blues. I used to go into the States to hear it, but all those blues players were coming up across the border anyway. Then we got to hear the way blues was really played. We still had our own interpretation, because we learned it on our own, influenced by the American Black musicians. Now the way we play is almost the same as them, but it still has our edge.

There are all kinds of blues: British blues, Delta blues, country blues and Chicago blues. And the Maritime blues! Toronto has its own blues sound. Blues is blues, but in each place the blues has its own little ring to it. The farther west you go, especially Vancouver, the white guys are playing blues almost like the Black guys from the States. In Vancouver, they get to see them all the time, because they just come across from Seattle. Albert Collins, who died about a year ago, is my favourite. You play blues because you love it. It's all feeling.

I think the focus on East Coast music is fantastic. Back when we opened for B.B. King two or three times, the guys in his band would say, "What part of Texas are you guys from?" I'd say, "We're from Nova Scotia." Now you can go out there and say you're from Nova Scotia and people actually know where it is! It's just a plane flight away from wherever you're going. I love Nova Scotia. I know it sounds corny, but I do. When I get out on the road and see all the other places, I can't wait to get home. I'll never leave Nova Scotia. I was born here, I'll die here.

F A N   f a r e

Booking agent
Eastern Talent International Inc.,
P.O. Box 847, Station M,
Halifax, NS,
B3J 2V2;
(902) 423-0266 (phone);
(902) 423-0735 (fax);
etimusic@fox.nstn.ca (e-mail)

Website
http://www.ottawa.net/~alive/dutch.html

Sarah McLachlan

DENNIS KEELEY

Born in 1968, Sarah McLachlan has reached a level of artistic maturity that takes most artists years to attain. Since releasing *Touch* in 1988, the Halifax native has explored her own unique musical interests, indifferent to current trends and fads. Sarah's intimate vocals and moody, evocative songs convey a passionate honesty rarely found in today's music.

Sarah toured extensively in support of her first album and went on to release *Solace* in 1991. That recording catapulted her to international prominence.

"... astonishing strength and clarity ..." — *Rolling Stone*

"Sarah McLachlan will be around for a while ... Trust your ears."
— *The New York Daily News*

We Are Part of Everything and Everything Is Part of Us

"You can take the girl out of the Maritimes, but you can't take the Maritimes out of the girl." Or so says my friend Buffy Childerhose — bless her heart. She's from the Maritimes as well, although she lives in Montreal now. When I start acting in certain ways — like when I have a beer and burp — she says, "Lord thunderin', girl," and brings me back down to earth.

I consider myself from the East Coast. Many people in the Maritimes "dis" me because I left. They don't consider me one of their own. National newspapers always say I'm from Vancouver. I'm always very clear to say I'm from Nova Scotia, but it never seems to get into print. So there's a perception that I'm not from the East Coast. I lived in Halifax. I grew up there. I spent nineteen years of my life in Halifax. How could it not be embedded in me?

My parents are both from the Western United States. My dad, who is a scientist, got his first job in Woods Hole, in Cape Cod, Massachusetts. His work took the family to the National Research Centre in Halifax. That was before I was born. My mom and dad have been there for more than thirty years now.

My early musical influences came mostly from my mother, who listened to people like Joan Baez, Cat Stevens, Simon and Garfunkel. My dad listened to a lot of classic jazz. That's what I grew up with.

For a while, I listened to AM radio, but in my teens I was into English New Wave. When I hit high school in the early 1980s, that whole New Wave thing took us by storm. Like Peter Gabriel (well, not that Peter Gabriel is New Wave), Kate Bush, Cocteau Twins, New Order, Depeche Mode, that whole scene. Then, of course, there was the punk phase when I was hanging out with punk rockers, listening to Black Flag, The Dead Kennedys, all that stuff. But that was more a fashion thing for me. I liked the people and so I hung out with them and happened to hear the music. Around

---

opening notes

Date of birth
January 28, 1968

Place of birth
Halifax, Nova Scotia

Language
English

Current residence
Vancouver, British Columbia

Instruments
Vocals, guitar, piano

> "My home is where my friends are."

the same time I joined a band called the October Game, which was doing mostly original tunes. In Halifax that was always a challenge. At that point there was only one venue, the Club Flamingo, where you could play new material as opposed to being a cover band. Through the years that I lived there, and to today, Greg Clark, who owns and operates the club, has always tried to promote original music. He is a tireless supporter of the Halifax music world.

I started taking ukulele lessons when I was four, and then I started taking classical guitar when I was seven because I wanted to be Joan Baez! Classical guitar was the only choice at the time. No one was teaching folk guitar. I got my musical training from the Maritime Conservatory of Music — twelve years of classical guitar. I went to Grade Seven or Eight, then I studied with Carol Van Fegglin at Dalhousie University. Classical guitar was a means to an end for me.

Once I hit fourteen I decided I didn't need lessons any more — which is probably very typical. My mother and father said, "We've invested all this money and you're bloody well going to continue." I'm not sure what they expected. I think they thought playing guitar was a lovely hobby. They were both academics and expected me and my brothers to go to university and excel in a field. I don't think they expected a concert classical guitarist. I always knew that music would lead me elsewhere. It was my passion: that and my art. But once I hit high school, I really lost interest in institutionalized learning. There were only a few teachers who had any passion for what they were doing.

select discography

- **Touch**/Nettwerk, 1988
- **Solace**/Nettwerk, 1991
- **Drawn to the Rhythm** (single)/Nettwerk, 1992
- **Fumbling Toward Ecstasy**/Nettwerk, 1993
- **Possession** (single)/Nettwerk, 1993
- **The Freedom Sessions** (CD+MM)/Nettwerk, 1994
- **B-Sides, Rarities and Other Stuff**/Nettwerk, 1996

I couldn't wait to get out of Halifax. I was feeling smothered and yearned for the bright lights and the big city and the glamour. I think a lot of people have that feeling about the place they grew up in. I moved to Vancouver, because my record company, Nettwerk, was there, and because I just needed a change.

Now, the more I go back to Halifax, the more I see what it really is, as opposed to my screwed-up vision of it at nineteen. Halifax held both negatives and positives for me. Luckily most of it now is positive. I come home at least twice a year to visit my mom and dad or to work. I much prefer just visiting Mom and Dad, because, when I have to work, I'm usually in and out in one day and there are about a billion people I want to see. A few of my close friends still live in Halifax — people I've maintained ties with for the past fifteen years. That's pretty amazing, considering I'm gone most of the time.

There has always been a lot of great music coming out of Nova Scotia and the Maritimes, but there has been no outlet for it and very few places to be seen within the community. I am so happy to see that situation changing. Now there is something called "the East Coast music scene." I think there always was, but we didn't ever get to hear about it. Now because there is more focus on it, bands feel they can try things, whereas before it seemed daunting. It was like "what's the point?"

My home is where my friends are, where I feel comfortable, and right now that's Vancouver. I grew up in Halifax and it's a huge part of my heritage — I'm not denying that by any stretch of the imagination — but wherever I feel comfortable at the time, that's my home. But anything's possible: I might return to the East.

I love the Maritimes, I love Halifax. I can't say anything negative about it any more. All that stuff is long gone. I can only say that growing up there shaped me and moulded me into who I am. And I am very happy with who I am.

FANfare

Management
Terry McBride & Dan Fraser,
Nettwerk Management;
(604) 654-2929 (phone);
(604) 654-1993 (fax);
info@nettwerk.com (e-mail)

Matt Minglewood

Although Matt Minglewood has been playing professionally for more than thirty years, he is still one of Canada's busiest touring artists. This singer/songwriter/guitarist has nine albums to his credit — two of them gold. He's had two Juno nominations, two Canadian Country Music nominations, and was named Canadian Country Music Songwriter of the Year in 1986 for his song "Me and the Boys." In 1990 he was honoured with a Lifetime Achievement Award at the ECMAs. He has also produced albums for Minglewood Band and *Cape Breton Summertime Revue*. He describes his music as a collage of country, rock and blues.

Something That Spoke to Me

My father and mother are both from Cape Breton. My family name is Batherson. My dad worked in Moncton in the CN yard until shortly after I was born, when they moved back to North Sydney. There were eight of us kids, and three cousins who lived with us permanently for years. There was a whack of us!

My grandfather was a fiddle player. My folks didn't play anything, but my father was a great whistler, a Scottish whistler. On my mom's side, they are all Scottish singers and dancers. I took violin lessons from Grade Six to Eight. That's as long as I lasted, but I never stopped singing or playing. I went from that to piano, then to guitar. I always sang. I sang my first concert when I was four.

My first professional gig was when I was in Grade Ten or so. We had a basement band called the Bell Tones because we had only one amp, and it was a Bell Tone. A guy gave us this hall for a percentage. The only people who showed up were three paying customers and two guys from another band I use to hang around with. That was the only gig that band ever did. But the band that was there to hear us liked what I was doing, and I started sitting in with them. There were no bars in North Sydney back then. We played Friday and Saturday night at the Kinsmen Centre and at high-school dances. There were two singers, me and Jimmy Hiscott. He did all the pop hits of the day, the top-forty stuff, and I did the bluesy stuff.

I grew up on R&B and blues. I played with a guy from the Black community down on the pier. That's the kind of music we did, their music. We used to play in the Club Unusual in Halifax, down on Creighton Street. It was an all-Black club, run by Bucky Adams and Joe Seeley. Then Sam Moon turned me on to the British stuff — John Mayall, Clapton, then the Animals. "House of the Rising Sun" and that kind of thing. We started searching back to the roots of the Black-American blues tradition. From first hearing it, I heard something that spoke to me. I just loved it.

opening notes

Date of birth
January 31, 1947

Place of birth
Moncton, New Brunswick

Current residence
Glace Bay, Cape Breton (NS)

Instruments
Vocals, guitar, keyboards, harmonica

> "There's a blues tradition in the Maritimes because we live a hard life here."

Minglewood was a joke that stuck. Sam Moon (whose name is really Richard Boudreau) had a band and I was in a band in North Sydney. We talked about putting a band together and going on the road. When we put the band together, those guys gave me the name Minglewood and it stuck. Minglewood comes from a Grateful Dead song, "The New, New Minglewood Blues." They changed my first name too because Roy didn't sound right with Minglewood. The band was called Sam Moon, Matt Minglewood and the Universal Power.

For about three or four years, Sam and I toured the country from one end to the other, but we didn't get any record deals, because we were too different. Sam was doing R&B and folk music and I was doing the blues. Eventually we split up. He went on to his thing and I went on to mine. The Minglewood band started recording in 1975.

I've been at it for over thirty years. I wouldn't do it if I didn't enjoy the music. I love playing. I'm going on fifty, and I'm not about to switch careers, but I never would have continued if I didn't enjoy it.

I've often been asked to leave the Maritimes for my career — not by people from here, although there're a few people who would probably like to see me go! I've been asked to move to Toronto or somewhere else by managers and record companies. But I just couldn't do it. I couldn't leave. I wanted my kids to grow up here and I wanted their roots to be here.

select discography

- **The Red Album**/independent, 1975
- **Minglewood Band**/RCA, 1979
- **Movin'**/RCA, 1980
- **M5**/CBS, 1984
- **Me and the Boys**/Savannah Records, 1986
- **The Promise**/Savannah Records, 1988
- "Forty-five Years From Now" and "Workin Joe" on **Stan Rogers: An East Coast Tribute, Vols. 1 & 2**/Atlantica/Duckworth, 1995

I think there's a blues tradition in the Maritimes because we live a hard life here and people identify with the music. We have the same sort of people as in the southern United States — the redneck, hard-working blue-collar type. People dumped on folks from the South as being backward and not quite hip. We've always had that handle too. The Maritimes has always had hard-living, hard-drinking, hard-partying, hard-working people. It's the same as in the South, where the blues came from.

Blues is not all that I do. A lot of the success I've had was not with straight-ahead blues. It was more like southern rock. What is nowadays called country is what I was doing ten or fifteen years ago: hard-edged, southern, Travis Tritt-style music. My early albums were all about that. It's been said many times that I was ten years ahead of my time.

There has always been a closeness among musicians here in the Maritimes — and I include Newfoundland in that too — in terms of musicians hanging around and exploring different kinds of music. Even among the rockers in the early days there was always a healthy competition, but a respect as well for each other's work. I think even today it spills over into the "Gaelic surge." Some of the guys who are playing Celtic music now have been playing rock all their lives. I know a keyboard player who played with the Oatley band and Rocked Out and ended up playing in Rita MacNeil's band.

I say, "to thine own self be true." You have to go with your feelings and be true to your music. You have to keep the spirit alive and keep at it, because if it doesn't happen today, it may tomorrow. And even if it doesn't ever happen, you still have to be true to what you are.

FANfare

Management
Grant Leslie,
P.O. Box 807,
Wolfville, NS,
B0P 1X0;
(902) 681-1342 (phone/fax)

Fan club
Matt Minglewood,
136 Main Street,
Glace Bay, NS,
B1A 4Y7

Modabo

Modabo, a New Brunswick-based acoustic trio, has touched audiences from Halifax to Toronto with their blend of musicianship, wit and original compositions. Their versatility enables them to please both theatre audiences and the pub crowd. Their debut recording, *Modabo*, led to two nominations at the 1996 ECMAs. They have played at numerous folk festivals across Canada and have a new album for release in 1997. Their quirky sense of humour does not overshadow their social conscience and contribution to their community.

"One would go far and wide to find better vocal harmonies than those produced by these three voices." — *The Evening Patriot*, Charlottetown

Left to right: Darrell, Mike, Jon

Doing Our Own Thing

Mike: Modabo evolved out of kitchen parties back home. We all had day jobs and other musical interests, and we would get together on weekends. Once friends who were graduating from the University of New Brunswick invited us to play on the *Pioneer Princess*. We took the gig, even though we ended up having to repeat a few tunes. We got another gig and we kept going from there.

Jon: We're all, for the most part, self-trained. I took about three years of piano in elementary school and flute lessons for a month, but I gave them up.

Darrell: My dad gave me a guitar when I was five, and I wouldn't have anything to do with it. I started off playing electric guitar when I was fifteen. Deep Purple was really important to me. I started listening to Rush and KISS. But as time went on, I started playing acoustic guitar more. I was never very good at figuring out other people's music, so I had to make up my own stuff.

Mike: My first group was a "do-wap" high-school group. Then I joined a rock 'n' roll band and was with them for two years. After that I joined a top-forty group and I was with them for five years. I've also sung in choirs and at weddings and I love to do karaoke. It's not for everybody, but it sure works for me. I love it.

My influences growing up were big bands. We lived with our grandparents for three years, and we got exposed to all this wonderful music, like Eddy Arnold, Vera Lynn and the Mills Brothers. I discovered that I had an interest in harmony and beat and spent most of my time developing my voice and my style — high end and falsetto. I did some theatre, some musicals. I love to sing the blues. I love country. I love classical music. All of it.

Jon: I grew up listening to hand-me-down albums of my older siblings: Bruce Cockburn; Joni Mitchell; Crosby, Stills and Nash. I

---

opening notes

Mike Doyle
Date of birth
August 17, 1965

Place of birth
Saint John, New Brunswick

Darrell Grant
Date of birth
May 17, 1961

Place of birth
Miramichi, New Brunswick

Jon Weaver
Date of birth
December 30, 1962

Place of birth
Montreal, Quebec

All
Current residence
Fredericton, New Brunswick

MAKING MUSIC

Mike Doyle
Vocals

Darrell Grant
Acoustic & electric guitar, vocals

Jon Weaver
Acoustic guitar, flute, keyboards, percussion, vocals

"There is a real sense of community."

sang in church choirs growing up. I listened to Genesis a lot. Hard rock, yes! I love the blues and jazz. Since I grew up in Montreal, the summer was always full of jazz and blues. I played in a blues band off and on for seven years in Fredericton.

Mike: One of our policies is, if we're not having fun, then we're just not in it. So we try to keep the communications lines open, and if there is a problem, we talk about it.

Jon: It is very much like a marriage, but without any sex.

Darrell: I'm not a political writer. I don't make many social statements. I like to look for individual situations, incidents, particular kinds of feelings, ones that many people experience.

Mike: Our new album is called *The Many and the One*. We're also hoping to do a couple of videos for that CD as well.

Jon: We recorded it on our own, in our living rooms and bedrooms and friends' basements. We went from there to the studios in Ontario. It shows a development from our last one. We were all quite happy in general about the first one, but the second one is a little more adventurous, a little more diversified in style. It's got everything, from a production pared down to a single guitar and a single voice to full-blown drums and bass, and lots of things in between.

Darrell: People have allowed me do my own thing in Fredericton. People pull for each other. You need friends, and you meet very helpful people along the way. There aren't a lot of people setting up impediments to what I want to do.

Jon: Even the more successful bands are very supportive of the up-and-coming bands. There is a real sense of community. I don't know if it's particular to the East Coast, but there's also a real history of

discography

- **Modabo**/Modabo Promotions, 1995
- **The Many and the One**/Modabo Promotions, 1997 release

kitchen party music and traditional music. It shows stylistically. The attitude is more of a happy "get together and collaborate and make music" than a "well, I can play this faster than you can." I think that is something from the Maritimes as well.

Mike: People from the East Coast appreciate what they have in terms of a community and in terms of the region. It really is a beautiful part of the world. It's like the Far East of the western world. Being near all this water gives such a sense of freedom and space.

FAN fare

Management
Mary Jago,
MJ Management,
5187 Sackville St., 2nd Floor,
Halifax, NS,
B3J 1K5;
(902) 429-9005 (phone);
(902) 429-9071 (fax);
modabo@nbenet.nb.ca (e-mail)

Website
http://www.ri-studios.com/modabo/mohome.html

Just Walk Right In

Jon: The first time we played in Halifax, we stayed with a good friend of ours. We didn't have a chance before we went to the gig to visit her, but she gave us directions. She'd said, "There are two houses side by each. I will leave the door open. My dog has been sick, so there might be sort of a gross animal smell. There will be a place on the main floor and a place in the basement." After the gig we went searching for the place. We tried the door, but it was locked. So we went to the place next door. Sure enough the door was open, except the place was a real mess. It was just in shambles, and it smelled awful. But she had warned us about that. Darrell crashed on the couch upstairs. There were some covers and a pillow there for him. I went down to the basement, and sure enough there was a bed down there. I stripped down to my skivvies and hopped into bed. The smell was so bad that it took me a while to get to sleep. Then I heard these footsteps coming down the stairs. I assumed it was our friend's fiancé, whom I had never met. He walked in, leaned over and clicked on the light. He was so shocked to see me he clicked off the light and panicked. Then he clicked it back on again and said, "What's this all about?"

As it turns out, we were in the wrong place, the neighbour's house. We didn't want to wake our friend, so we tried to sleep in the back of the VW bus we had borrowed. Since we were parked on a rather steep incline, we had trouble getting to sleep. Part of the trouble was that we kept sliding toward our feet, but mostly it was because every time there was a little bit of silence one of us would break into laughter.

Anne Murray

With one of the most immediately recognizable voices in popular music, Anne Murray is a singer's singer. Her achievements are most impressive: four Grammy Awards, two American Music Awards, twenty-five Juno Awards, as well as a place in the Juno Hall of Fame. Her latest release, simply titled *Anne Murray*, is her thirtieth album. What has made Anne Murray so successful? Anne has a soulful voice that takes a song and makes it into a musical poem. She exudes charisma, charm and a down-to-earth sensibility. Anne Murray is truly one of the Maritimes' favourite daughters.

JAMES O'MARA

Ties to Home

I grew up in Springhill, Nova Scotia. I can't think of any place I would rather be from — probably because it's home for me. Springhill had two major mining disasters and, although my childhood was very happy, the town's tragic history shaped it in a way. At a very young age, I saw things a lot of people don't. I saw the resilience of people who live every day with the threat of death, and I must have drawn some strength from all of that. I also saw the Maritimers' and Newfoundlanders' sense of humour. Their sense of humour put these people above their difficulties. That self-deprecating, subtle sense of humour has stayed with me forever. It's part of my stage show, and a big part of the success of my career, I think. In some places it is understood better than in others. In places like Australia and New Zealand, people catch on in a second, in a heartbeat. All of a sudden there is that bond there: they get it. But, even in some parts of Canada, it takes people a little longer to get it.

I came from a doctor's family, and we were never without anything, but I certainly saw those who were. My father had a very dry, sardonic sense of humour. It could cut you to the quick with very few words, but in a way that you weren't hurt. My brothers still do it to this day. They just tear each other to shreds, and me too. I have five brothers. I was treated as one of the boys. I didn't ever get away with anything because I was a girl, that's for sure.

I don't know what it is about the Maritimes — maybe it's the ocean — I just know it's there. There's a great line from "Please Don't Sell Nova Scotia," a song I did years ago, written by Peter Cornell, who later changed his name to Peter Pringle. The line is "What seems like only a piece of ground gets into your blood and turns your heart around."

I had no choice but to move. I don't see how I could have stayed in the Maritimes and made it happen. There were no studios at that

---

opening notes

Date of birth
June 20, 1945

Place of birth
Springhill, Nova Scotia

Heritage
Scottish/Acadian

Language
English

Current residence
Toronto, Ontario

Instruments
Vocals, guitar

> "I am welcomed [home] with open arms."

time, and all the television was in Toronto. But, believe you me, I didn't want to move. I was so scared; my impressions of Toronto had not been the greatest. I remember the first time I came to Toronto. I was doing a television show, and, because I was from the Maritimes, the make-up people were looking down their noses at me. "Are you from that Don Messer show?" they asked, and I said no. They used to think that show was, like, from Hicksville, yet it was the most successful television show this country has ever produced. I wasn't from that show, but that was the attitude I encountered. But I had no choice: either I was going to pursue my career or not. I remember travelling back and forth doing the *Glen Campbell Goodtime Hour*. I had these two tickets a month that would take me from Halifax to Los Angeles, and it would take all day to get there.

So I moved. The television and recording studios were in Toronto, and some really fine musicians. At that time we were all learning. There were no music managers. Leonard Rambeau, who took over managing me in 1977, had learned everything he knew from managers in the United States.

Things have changed since then. The world is getting smaller. In the Maritimes now we have studios; we have people who can produce; we have musicians; we have all of that. The talent was always there, but it was just a matter of developing them. George Hebert, my guitar player, lives in Halifax. When he travels with me, he just flies out of Halifax to wherever we are. It's more of a global village now. It might be possible to live in the Maritimes now and have a big career. I don't know.

select discography

- **There's a hippo in my tub**/Capital Records, 1977
- **Croonin'**/EMI Music Canada, 1993
- **Best of the Season**/EMI Music Canada, 1994
- **Now & Forever**/EMI Music Canada, 1994
- **The Best ... So Far**/EMI Music Canada, 1994
- **Anne Murray**/EMI Music Canada, 1996

I spend at least a month in Nova Scotia in the summer. I would like to make it more. Some summers I do, others I don't. Every time I fly into Moncton or Halifax, everyone says, "Hi, Anne." It's truly like going home. Maritimers claim me as one of their own, and rightly so, because that's the way I feel too. They are happy that I have succeeded; I am welcomed with open arms and treated as if I never left. But if I lived there, I wouldn't have this light at the end of the tunnel every year. It keeps me going for the whole year. It never goes away. Maritimers are tied to their home and want to go back. Each time I do go home, it's never long enough, and it tears my heart out when I leave. I will always yearn to go back.

FANfare

Manager
Bruce Allen Talent,
406 - 68 Water Street,
Vancouver, BC,
V6B 1A4;
(604) 688-7274 (phone);
(604) 688-7118 (fax)

Booking agent (U.S.)
Fred Laurence, ICM,
Los Angeles, CA

Fan club
The Anne Murray
International Fan Club,
P.O. Box 118, Madison Centre,
4950 Yonge Street,
Toronto, ON,
M2N 6K1

Website
http://www.annemurray.com/am

Breakaway Pants

Once I was performing in a pair of breakaway pants, long pants with Velcro seams that I could rip off when I did my dance number. They were beautiful, sequined pants, and no one would expect they would be coming off. Well, the pants fell in the second number of the show. They hadn't been fastened properly and they just fell right down to my ankles. Of course I had a pair of fancy shorts underneath, but it was like having a pair of pantyhose around my ankles. I couldn't move. I motioned to Debbie Ankeny, my back-up singer, to come over and help me, but she was laughing so hard she couldn't do it. And the band, by this time, were all on their faces, they were laughing so hard. Finally, I had to stop the song, and say, "I guess you folks are wondering what my pants are doing around my ankles." I made it into a big production and people thought it was part of the show. Dropping my pants — that was a career highlight.

Nova Scotia Mass Choir

Since its debut in 1992, the Nova Scotia Mass Choir, one of the only multiracial gospel choirs in North America, continues to stir the souls of audiences at home and abroad. The choir, which boasts members from across Nova Scotia, were honoured to be the only Canadian gospel choir to perform at the thirtieth-anniversary celebrations of the Martin Luther King March on Capital Hill in Washington, DC, in 1993. Through its performances, the choir shares its love of gospel music and promotes cross-cultural understanding.

"They are our finest ambassadors, promoting racial harmony and encouraging others to follow their example."

— Walter Fitzgerald, Mayor, Halifax Regional Municipality

Praising the Lord through Song
[Interview with Linda Carver]

I have been the president of the Nova Scotia Mass Choir since its inception in 1992, and I am also one of the soloists. In that year, an international gospel festival in Halifax needed a choir to back up a number of artists. We became that choir. It was a mixed bag of people who came together by word of mouth: teachers, doctors and lawyers; singers from Halifax, Dartmouth, East and North Preston; and people of different ages, including three mother-daughter teams, of which my daughter and I are one. After the festival, we were supposed to disband because we were formed just for it, but we liked the mix, decided to form a society, and here we are today. We have a waiting list of people interested in joining and we invite them to come to the rehearsals and listen in. When we have spaces come up in the choir, we call upon those people to see if they are able to make the commitment to join the choir.

There are about sixty-three members, most of whom were in the choir when it formed in 1992. Our membership criteria are that you agree to come to rehearsals and performances — the big ones and the small ones. We're not trained singers, and the majority of us do not read music. We learn the material by ear. Most of our music is gospel music, both traditional and modern, but we also do other selections that talk about people coming together in a peaceful manner. We change the words of a jazz or blues song and turn it into a gospel song. A couple of people in the choir direct us, along with outside directors, like Woody Woods from Las Vegas.

As a youth, I spent some time in the choir at my Baptist church, and for about three years in my twenties I sang with a group that performed throughout the Maritimes. After I had my first child, I found I couldn't do it any more. I missed the infant so much when

opening notes

Sopranos
Mary Adams, Sonia Adams, Lela Colley, Chris Crooks, Deborah Deleon, Jennifer Dingle, Valerie Dixon, Lenora Downey, Sharon Earle, Brenda Fenn, Carolyn Fowler, Belinda Grant, Janice Grant, Tanya Howe, Dawn Matthews-Nichols, Eileen Ouelette, Wendy Shea, Sandra Slawter, Deanna Sparks, Colleen Symonds, Luvina Thomas, Cecily Williams, Darcel Williams-Hart

Altos
Lorraine Buchan, Tina Carvery, Shelley Fashan, Rosella Fraser, Karen Grant, Kathy Grant, Shauntay Grant, Elizabeth Guildford, Charlotte Harper, Kim Harper, Mary Ann MacKinnon-Boyd, Kim MacLeod, Cynthia Murray, Maureen O'Connell, Lucille Robinson, Viki Samuels-Stewart, Verona Singer, Helen Vaughan, Iesha Williams

(more ...)

opening notes

Tenors
Stephanie Bruce, Linda Carvery, Joseph Colley, Blair Haverstock, Sharon Johnson, Beverly Lewis, Carman Nelson, Joy O'Brien, June Ross, Sue Taylor

Basses
Michael Bailey, Dan Blunden, Ken Boyd, Thelma Coward-Ince, Clark Cromwell, Tim Edmonds, Larry Patterson, Jeremiah Sparks

Band members
Bruce Chapman, piano; Gary Steed, drums; Bucky Adams, saxophone; John Theodore, organ; Bruce Jacobs, bass; John Chaisson, bass

> "The music is energizing, joyful, powerful."

I was away that I stopped for about twenty years. I started again during the International Gospel Festival and have stayed with the choir ever since.

Being in the group has really helped me understand people better, because I've had to work with really diverse people. The music is energizing, joyful, powerful. It almost reminds me of the feelings that a person would have within a family structure, all the tension, happiness, sadness and anger that are part of it.

We've toured twice in the United States, and in 1993 we took part in the Southern Christian Leadership Convention, which coincided with the thirtieth anniversary of the March on Washington. The American people seemed fascinated that the Mass Choir, a group of people of mixed races, sang together and travelled together from so far away. It was something that they just don't see a whole lot. We were the only mixed choir that took part in any of their festivities. One of the directors from Las Vegas who worked with us said, "With American gospel choirs, the accent is basically the same, but within the Mass Choir, you have one accent coming from North Preston, another from Cape Breton, and still another from Newfoundland. When you mix them all together, what a unique sound!" He had never heard that all blended together in a gospel choir and he found it really intriguing.

To get to Washington, we travelled by bus for some thirty hours (because the driver got lost). That's a long time to be travelling in intense heat, with your feet swollen by the time you get off the bus. We sang a lot on the bus, even though we're not supposed to. I remember the director saying, "You have to keep your voices intact," but we just felt like talking and singing and we were just having a wonderful time. But by the time we got there, there were a couple of people who had towels around their necks; they couldn't perform. But that's just the way it goes, and you learn your lessons.

discography

- **He Never Failed Me Yet**/Jongleur Productions, 1996

We produced our first CD, *He Never Failed Me Yet*, in the spring of 1996 and performed in the new CBC-TV production *Hallelujah* that will be seen on Vision TV and on the CBC. We hope to use some of the material we recorded for that production as part of our second CD.

East Coast music is a mixed bag of musical talents within the Maritimes. Promoters on the East Coast are starting to recognize other aspects of music here. That's where we come in. Our community recognizes the choir as a good thing, and appreciates that the combination of faiths and races is very powerful. It is seen that way not only in the Black community, but also in the white community. Audiences tell us that we demonstrate a feeling of peacefulness and togetherness. We seem to exude it during our performances. I take that as a great compliment.

Gospel music certainly brings out or expands a person's level of spirituality. I find that one can not venture too far in a wonderful way without a certain amount of true faith. There's a great deal of joy and spirituality within the choir, and a sense of freedom. We just let it loose. Normally, I don't spend a lot of time talking; singing helps me express myself, whether it's my anger, frustration, happiness or whatever. I think this sense of freedom comes with time.

A person has to have a sense of freedom to be able to do what they really like to do and do it the best they can. The audience will pick that up. You don't have to say a word; the audience will respond. If you truly want to do something and the sense of freedom is there and all the inhibitions are gone, you do it just beautifully, in my opinion.

FANfare

Management
The Executive, NS Mass Choir
2151 Gottingen Street,
P.O. Box 47031,
Halifax, NS,
B3K 5Y2

Bookings
Lucille Robinson,
221 Victoria Road,
Dartmouth, NS,
B3A 1W5;
(902) 466-7653 (phone);
(902) 455-3856 (fax)

Scott Parsons

PAUL FLETCHER

Scott Parsons calls his unique blend of folk, blues and reggae "Rastacadian." This talented singer/songwriter/guitarist has proven international appeal. He and his band, Jupiter Wise, have toured Switzerland twice and performed across Canada, the United States and Mexico. In 1994 his autobiographical song "What I Am" was chosen as the theme song for the United Nations Convention on the Rights of the Child. Scott is the founder and producer of the Annual Gene MacLellan Music Festival held in Victoria, Prince Edward Island, which pays tribute to one of Canada's foremost songwriters.

"[Jupiter Wise] is not just a good first album, but an outstanding album."

— *Mainstreet* (CBC Radio), Prince Edward Island

What I Am

I've lived all over Canada because my father was in the military. My mother's mother is part Mi'kmaq from Pubnico, Nova Scotia, and her father was from Nottingham, England. My father's people are Black and came from Lucasville, Nova Scotia. They were free, not slaves. My great-great-grandfather was from Scotland, which is where the name Parsons came from.

In elementary school I started playing a ukulele. Once I got my hands on this little string unit, I just kept playing. I played it until Grade Five or so. There were guitars in my house. My older brother and my father play guitar, and I started when I was about thirteen. Mark, a younger brother, has a degree in classical trumpet.

There was a musical group, the Troubadours, which performed at the Confederation Centre in Charlottetown, PEI, every day for a few summers. They couldn't get rid of me once I had a guitar and had learned a few songs. Actually, they were quite encouraging and let me play. Lucien Laroux was a really major influence on me. When I was a kid, I followed him around and tried to learn the guitar. And Gene MacLellan was another. I used to hitchhike out to Gene's house in the country. He'd let me hang around and listen to all these musicians he would always have there.

Jean Desroches also had a big influence on me. She lives here in Charlottetown, and writes songs and plays. She ran a boarding house, and everyone there seemed to play music. I was always drawn to blues. Taj Mahal's "Giant Step" is a great song, and I think he did the best solo set I've ever seen anyone do. Bob Marley is one of my favourite musicians. So is David Lindley, an incredible guitar player and musician.

I'm not a studied musician. I play by ear. I read music like a snail. I'm driven to play music. It satisfies something inside me that money and material things don't even touch. I have always been drawn to music. I'm in my element when I'm playing music and performing.

---

opening notes

Date of birth
September 19, 1958

Place of birth
Picton, Ontario

Heritage
Afro-Canadian, Mi'kmaq, English, Scottish

Language
English

Current residence
Charlottetown, Prince Edward Island

Instruments
Guitar, vocals

> "I'm driven to play music."

Jupiter Wise, the name of my band, comes from a story about a slave here in Prince Edward Island who found this strange plea on the law books called "Yea benefit of clergy." After assaulting a slave owner, he used this plea to save himself from being hanged, and instead was sent on a slave ship to the West Indies for seven years of hard labour. I read some of this story in a book called *Black Islanders* by Jim Hornby. The Black community on PEI certainly had an influence on this place. Slavery was still here in Prince Edward Island a little after it was abolished in the States. Slaves were running from here to the Northern States to get away from it.

I write from personal experience about issues that affect me, about human equality more than just racial equality. The United Nations used my song "What I Am," which talks about my background, as the theme song for the youth conference at the Rights of the Child Conference in 1994. That was quite an honour. The song says that there is already enough pain and trouble in the world, without people creating it.

Some of my country songs probably reflect a Maritime influence from growing up here and from playing Celtic music. I also like to play reggae and blues and rock. I try not to limit myself. I call the music I play "Rastacadian" because of all of these influences. Perhaps if I stuck to one genre of music I would be more successful. I've had my band over in Switzerland twice in the last two years. We had a great time there. People really respond well to us.

I'm pretty much rooted here in the Maritimes. I would like to see people support the East Coast music a lot more. There's a lot of potential here. In a way, it's nice that Prince Edward Island is a bit removed from the mainstream. Things develop a little slower, but they end up being a lot nicer because of the pace of life here. There are always limitations to living in a remote place. I could

discography

- **Jupiter Wise**/independent, 1993
- **Live at Magahony Hall**/independent, 1995

The Idle Wild

I was playing one time in British Columbia in a bar called the Idle Wild. We were staying above the tavern, and about noon we heard what sounded like an earthquake going on downstairs. These logging trucks with all these loggers pulled in because it was too wet for them to work. They were incredibly rowdy. That night on stage we were probably a little bit loud, and these giant loggers were hammered drunk. One guy took his chair by the arms, bent over, and ran the full length of the bar, driving his head right into our speaker, which was huge. We had all kinds of harmonicas and glasses and stuff like that stacked on top of it. The whole thing rocked and then fell over. We thought the logger had knocked himself out, but he got up and threw a chair across the stage, knocking over everything else. The RCMP arrived and said, "Jesse, you're drunk. Go home." Jesse got in his truck and drove away.

The next morning, we met the logger at the RCMP station. The police told us to just go and have a coffee somewhere and figure out how much he should pay us for all the broken gear. The guy apologized, but didn't even remember what he'd done. When we were leaving town, we saw another band arriving in their van. They were glam rockers with make-up and nice hairdos. As we were driving by them, we just yelled, "Good luck, boys."

work more steadily if I lived in Toronto. I've lived across Canada and travelled in the States, Europe and Mexico, but Prince Edward Island is where I want to live.

FANfare

Management/bookings
Scott Parsons,
21 Chestnut Street,
Charlottetown, PEI,
C1A 1Z5;
(902) 892-4084 (phone);
design@virtuo.com (e-mail)

Website
http://www.virtuo.com/music/scott.html

The Rankin Family

The Rankins all play music — all twelve of them. But the five the world knows as the Rankin Family have been playing together since the late 1980s. In just a few years they have taken their unique Celtic-influenced music to the top of the Canadian charts and around the world. And their fans have contributed to sales of more than one million records in Canada and made them one of Canada's most successful groups. They have been nominated for and won more East Coast Music Awards than anyone else in the awards' ten-year history. Many musicians would readily attribute the recent explosion of East Coast music to this amazing family group from Inverness County, Cape Breton.

Left to right: Raylene, Jimmy, Heather, Cookie, John Morris

Born into the Music

We've always played music. Our musical career began at home. Neighbours would gather every third weekend for a party, or *ceilidh*, as it is known in Gaelic. With our father on violin and mother on piano, the older children would learn Celtic dance steps and songs. As the older kids grew up and left, the younger ones would replace them.

We played at local weddings and dances. Part of the appeal we may have had was that we played a wide range of music and had a lot of different influences: country, Celtic, fiddle music. We sang harmonies, and we even played old rock 'n' roll stuff. It was music that would appeal to everyone at those dances. It's not as though we've changed our focus over the years. We've always dabbled in different types of music.

In 1989, the five of us — Cookie, Heather, Raylene, Jimmy and John Morris Rankin — were encouraged to perform at various folk festivals. Raylene handled most of the bookings, while our mother looked after mail orders for our two independent releases, *The Rankin Family* and *Fare Thee Well Love*.

Keeping Gaelic traditions alive and fresh is the heart of the band. It is the essence of Rankin music; that and the close harmonies. John Morris's style is traditional but unique in the sense that, if you're a good fiddler, over time you'll develop your own style. He comes out of the same tradition as Ashley MacIsaac, but the approaches are very different.

We aren't fluent in Gaelic, however, although we took Gaelic in school from Margie Beaton, and one of our relatives, Effie Rankin, helps with the Gaelic pronunciation.

All five of us have graduated from Nova Scotia-based post-secondary institutions. Jimmy has a fine arts degree from Nova Scotia's College of Art and Design in Halifax. St. Francis Xavier University in Antigonish has three of us as alumni: John Morris graduated in

---

opening notes

Cookie (nee Carol Jean)
Date of birth
May 4

Heather
Date of birth
October 24

Jimmy
Date of birth
May 28

John Morris
Date of birth
April 28

Raylene
Date of birth
September 15

For All
Place of birth
Mabou, Cape Breton (NS)

MAKING MUSIC

Cookie
Vocals, percussion

Heather
Vocals, piano, percussion

Jimmy
Vocals, acoustic guitar, percussion

John Morris
Vocals, piano, fiddle, guitar

Raylene
Vocals, percussion

"Keeping Gaelic traditions live and fresh is the heart of the band."

1980, Raylene in 1982 and Cookie in 1987. Cookie continued on to Acadia University in Wolfville, where she, along with Heather, was granted a Bachelor of Arts degree. Raylene followed up her BA with a law degree from Dalhousie in Halifax. All of us were recently awarded honorary music doctorates from Acadia University.

Raylene and Cookie: We think it's a gift. The last six years have been amazing. We couldn't have anticipated this kind of response, or that it would keep going on. It's exciting.

John Morris: I think we're learning to use the means that are available to expose what we have to offer. A lot of young musicians now know how to use all the media to get their product out there, to get their picture out there.

For us, winning the four Junos was a great thing; it was a tribute to the people who helped make it all happen. There were a lot of positive spin-offs to it, but it does put more pressure on a group or artist.

Jimmy: Part of the reason for our success is that we've allowed ourselves to be open to different influences and not be labelled as one particular thing. We're not a country band; we're not a Celtic band; we're not a folk band. We're a hybrid. We've crossed over a lot of barriers. That's what music's about, anyway.

We're going more in the direction of original writing. The traditional stuff obviously means a lot to us, but we're writing all the time and it's tough to hold our own songs back.

discography

- **The Rankin Family** (re-release)/EMI Music Canada, 1992
- **Fare Thee Well** (re-release)/EMI Music Canada, 1992
- **North Country**/EMI Music Canada, 1993
- **Grey Dusk of Eve** (EP, limited edition)/EMI Music Canada, 1995
- **Endless Seasons**/EMI Music Canada, 1995
- **Collection**/EMI Music Canada, 1996

I'm pretty disciplined about writing. But it's very important for me to be in the right spot. Your work will reflect your surroundings. I'm most comfortable at home, near the sea, having my down time. I guess I am a hopeless romantic.

Raylene: I started out as a solo performer, with different back-ups, mostly duo. It was a very different from what we have with the band. For one, there's no support system, or at least not the kind I need to thrive. From its inception, the band felt right. It's given me a range of experiences I doubt I would have had on my own. I might have had equally interesting ones, but I don't think on this scale or at this level. I feel that it was meant to be for me to be in the Rankin Family, and it's been just the most exceptional gift since.

Yet when you have five lead voices, it doesn't always mean that the person who brings in a song is the one who'll end up singing it. We decide that by a process of elimination — painful elimination. Even for us there can be such a thing as too much togetherness. It's not as bad now, because on tours we have our own rooms and have built our different relationships off the road. At the end of the tour, we all go our separate ways. But we all still live in Nova Scotia.

I think the recent success of East Coast musicians — and of Canadian music in general — had something to do with the confidence in the music. In the last five to ten years, the industry, more so than the public even, feels secure and confident in Canadian music. That effect has just spilled over to the East Coast. The music has always been there. There have always been people from the East Coast who've made it nationally and internationally, like Anne Murray, Rita MacNeil, Figgy Duff. There's been a kind of renaissance in the last five years.

One thing about East Coast people is that they have learned to laugh. The area has been stressed economically since the turn of the century. They learned not to take things so seriously and to enjoy what they have.

FAN fare

Management
Chip Sutherland/Mickey Quase,
Pier 21 Artist Management Ltd.,
5151 George Street, Suite 1701,
Halifax, NS,
B3J 1M5;
(902) 492-2100 (phone);
(902) 492-3738 (fax);
pier21@fox.nstn.ca (e-mail)

Fan club
Kaye Rankin,
P.O. Box 43,
Mabou, NS,
B0E 1X0

Website
http://www.chatsabo.com/rankins/

Rawlins Cross

With members from Newfoundland, Nova Scotia and Prince Edward Island, Rawlins Cross epitomizes the best of Atlantic-Canadian music, taking the Celtic folk music of the region into the contemporary world by fusing it with progressive sounds. Highland bagpipes, mandolin, accordion and bodhran drum combine with electric guitar, bass and drums for an exhilarating blend of highly danceable, original rock and stirring instrumental arrangements of traditional Celtic melodies.

Some of the band's more interesting gigs include the Milwaukee Irish Festival, opening for the Pogues, and the G-7 Summit in Halifax in 1995.

Left to right: Ian, Howie, Geoff, Joey, Brian, Dave

The Kings of Celtic Rock

Dave: My brother Geoff and I met Ian McKinnon in 1985, when he was living in St. John's. We played together on a casual basis for two or three years, then around 1988 we coined the name Rawlins Cross after an intersection in St. John's. After a couple of years and a couple of bass players, we hooked up with Brian Bourne, who I had known for a long time. He was the logical choice for bass player. Howie Southwood was one of the most in-demand drummers around town when we took him on board. Joey Kitson is the most recent addition. We heard him when he was singing for a tourism promotion. He's an amazing vocalist, so we decided to take him.

Ian: My grandmother played the piano and was a big influence in our family. There was always lots of Cape Breton fiddle and piano music around my grandparents' place. My dad was influenced by it, and so was I.

Geoff: There was always music around our house, too. My mother was a contralto in her day. She had the opportunity to study music but decided to get married and have kids instead. That was the style at the time. I started to pick up the Magnus Chord Organ that went through there in the late 1960s. I got one for Christmas when I was about twelve or thirteen. That's sort of where I started.

Dave: Our mother did a lot of work in musicals and choruses. And growing up in Newfoundland we were exposed to the Irish and the Newfoundland music that was around St. John's. It was almost impossible to avoid it.

Brian: I, on the other hand, grew up in Quebec and had a pop-music background. My older brother played guitar and had a Stones clone band in about 1965. I do have some musical blood way back. My great-aunt on my mom's side, Nina Gale, sang opera

opening notes

Brian Bourne
Date of birth
August 31, 1955

Place of birth
Thetford Mines, Quebec

Current residence
Halifax, Nova Scotia

Joey Kitson
Date of birth
November 23, 1969

Place of birth
Charlottetown,
Prince Edward Island

Current residence
Charlottetown,
Prince Edward Island

Ian McKinnon
Date of birth
November 27, 1961

Place of birth
Halifax, Nova Scotia

Current residence
Halifax, Nova Scotia

(more …)

opening notes

Dave Panting
Date of birth
February 12, 1956

Place of birth
Fort Churchill, Manitoba

Current residence
St. John's, Newfoundland

Geoff Panting
Date of birth
July 5, 1957

Place of birth
Fort Churchill, Manitoba

Current residence
St. John's, Newfoundland

Howie Southwood
Date of birth
May 28, 1954

Place of birth
Cape Town, South Africa

Current residence
Elora, Ontario

FANfare

Management
Ground Swell Production,
P.O. Box 245, Central Station,
Halifax, NS,
B3J 2N7;
(902) 492-0744 (phone);
(902) 492-0259 (fax)

---

at La Scala in Italy in 1925 and taught at the Royal Conservatory in Toronto for years after that.

With the differences in our musical backgrounds, we have a true fusion of tastes and styles — hence our "Celtic rock" label. There is some of the old and lots of the new. We're a real mess as far as trying to pin us down to one style. We have influences from the Saxons and from the Jamaicans, and there is quite a bit of Celtic in there too. We are truly a mishmash — a good combination of all those styles.

Dave: I think, being identified with the region we walk a tightrope. It has a down side if you are trying to reach a larger audience. Our music is slotted because of the Celtic content, but we really do a more original thing. It's somewhere in between for us. I mean I am very proud to be from Newfoundland. I am proud of the place. And I acknowledge that it has given me a musical identity that I never would have had growing up somewhere else. However, I try not to let that restrict me.

Ian: Here in the region, the general population thinks there is a thriving music scene, and, in fact, there is — here in the region. My parents have a hardware store in Port Hawkesbury, Cape Breton. People come in and want to know how I am spending my millions of dollars. The reality is that, even though our group and a lot of the other artists in the region enjoy a very high profile, we don't enjoy that same kind of profile across Canada and North America and around the world. It's still a struggle for most of us to perform and to play our music, and to sell records and maintain ourselves.

Geoff: I think people got hip to the fact that music is a business. The public in North America is ready for this particular style at

discography

- **A Turn of the Wheel**/Ground Swell/Warner, 1989
- **Crossing the Border**/Ground Swell/Warner, 1992
- **Reel 'n' Roll**/Ground Swell/Warner, 1993
- **Living River**/Ground Swell/Warner, 1996

the moment. Roots music is always popular, but these things tend to run in cycles. There was a folk revival in the early 1970s. Figgy Duff from Newfoundland had some real success for a while then. Those things tend to go around. My idea is to make hay while the sun shines. One person's success from this region draws attention to the region, and therefore it's everyone's success.

Dave: Now, because of the business set-up, younger bands can have a larger profile in a shorter time. Whether the longevity will be there remains to be seen.

Brian: Often after a gig we're invited out to a house party. People play music at these parties all night. That's a real tradition here and it doesn't seem to be fading. I don't think you find that all over Canada; at least, I haven't. The fiddles and pianos come out and the banjo and guitars and mandolins, and people play all night long. There's no better way to see that sun come up than having six or seven hours of music behind you.

MAKING MUSIC

Brian Bourne
Bass, Chapman Stick, back-up vocals

Joey Kitson
Lead vocals, harmonica

Ian McKinnon
Highland bagpipe, tin whistle, bodhran

Dave Panting
Guitar, mandolin, back-up vocals

Geoff Panting
Button & piano accordion, keyboards

Howie Southwood
Drums

In Devastation Channel

Ian: Our first big tour together as a band was a five-week marathon tour of small community concert venues in Alberta and British Columbia. One of those venues was a place called Kemano, near Kitimat, BC. In order to get to Kemano you have to either fly in by helicopter or be ferried in. We were taken over in small boat along with our two tons of gear and five band members and our soundman. The sound gear was strapped to the open deck.

It was a stormy snowy day in late November. We headed down Devastation Channel and were barely making headway when the waves started to lap up over the back deck over the gear. Our soundman was pulling his hair out. Then we hit a deadhead log, which ripped out the right engine of the boat. After about four or five hours, they sent the big boat out after us and towed us in.

The old adage about "the show must go on" proved true that night because we pulled it off. We got all the electronic equipment sorted out and dried off with several hair dryers. Then we got up on stage and played.

sandbox

The members of sandbox grew up together in New Glasgow, Nova Scotia. They hung out together, played hockey together and suddenly were making music together. Since becoming a band, sandbox recorded their debut album *bionic* and released "Curious" as the first single/video in Canada. The song was a hit on radio and was a top-ten video on MuchMusic. Soon after, sandbox hit the road and released another single/ video "Collide." *Bionic* is currently pushing gold status in Canada. Although all band members are in their early twenties, they are seasoned at touring and love the "road" as much as Jack Kerouac did.

Left to right: Jason, Mike, Troy, Paul, Scott

GORDON HAWKINS

An East Coast Attitude
[Interview with Mike Smith]

None of us took music too seriously until about two or three years ago. I taught myself to play guitar out of books and although I was always into music, I was also into hockey. Once I got out of hockey, I started putting a lot more time into music.

I was a huge fan of Rick Emmett from the Toronto band Triumph. In junior high, I thought he was God. Ever since I was little I've also been a huge Beatles fan. I like a lot of Canadian stuff too. The Rheostatics are one of my favourite bands. I like pretty much anything that's melody-oriented.

I don't think the East Coast influenced us musically so much. When the rest of Canada hears about the East Coast, they automatically think Celtic, but we were never into that kind of music.

It used to be that you had to be a Celtic band if you were from here and wanted be recognized anywhere. But about four or five years ago when Sloan and jale and Hardship Post started to get known internationally, it seemed possible to write music outside the Celtic tradition and get recognized for it.

We started the band as something to do in the summer. Scott MacFarlane had played in bands since he was twelve or thirteen, and Troy and Jay Archibald had played together for a long time. At first the band was more of a fun thing — not that it isn't fun now. Then in August 1993 we recorded a six-song EP in Halifax entitled *Maskman*. We got on the Indie charts in Halifax, and it climbed to number one on Sam the Record Man's charts. We thought it was pretty funny actually. Then we got signed to Latitude.

We put out our first album, *bionic*, in April 1995. At the same time, we released the song "Curious" as a video single. It went to number nine on MuchMusic. Since 1995, we've toured Canada four times and the shows kept getting better. Playing live is why we do what we do — that and the chance to make a few records.

opening notes

Jason (Jay) Archibald
Date of birth
August 21, 1971

Place of birth
Pictou, Nova Scotia

Current residence
New Galsgow, Nova Scotia

Scott MacFarlane
Date of birth
May 11, 1973

Place of birth
Halifax, Nova Scotia

Current residence
Westville, Nova Scotia

Paul Murray
Date of birth
April 9, 1971

Place of birth
New Glasgow, Nova Scotia

Current residence
New Glasgow, Nova Scotia

(more ...)

opening notes

Troy Shanks
Date of birth
June 12, 1971

Place of birth
Halifax, Nova Scotia

Current residence
New Glasgow, Nova Scotia

Mike Smith
Date of birth
August 27, 1972

Place of birth
New Glasgow, Nova Scotia

Current residence
Thorburn, Nova Scotia

"We just did our own thing really."

By the time we got about halfway through our first tour the video was really catching on. We could play in some town in British Columbia and get a good crowd because people knew who we were from MuchMusic. Before that we'd been playing clubs, but people had no idea who we were. It's depressing to play for nobody. We are totally grateful to MuchMusic and all the radio stations across Canada who play us.

Being from New Glasgow, we were never part of the Halifax Indie scene. When we'd go to Halifax to play, we would end up either being the only act or being on a bill with bands we didn't know. There is a band from Halifax called Milo (formerly the Purple Helmets), who are good friends of ours. We usually ended up playing with them mostly in Halifax. We stuck with them, but we did our thing and they did theirs. Both of our bands were isolated from the rest of the scene. We've been gone and they have been around so they might be more accepted in and around Halifax than we are. It wasn't a case of being like Rudolph, where we wanted to get in the scene but weren't accepted. It was more that we did our thing and just basically wrote the way we wanted to. We've always had the philosophy: "If it fits, it fits. If it doesn't, that's even better.

We have never put as much emphasis on succeeding, as some bands do. We never get our hopes up or count on going any further. We do take it seriously, but we are careful not to think that in two years we are going to be huge and have all this money and all these records. We do things the way we want to do them. If it sells and people like it, that's great. If it doesn't, so be it. What I mean is that we make records to satisfy ourselves primarily. If other people like it, that's just a bonus.

Anything that happens to me, good or bad, usually finds its way into something I write. I don't usually know what I'm going to write

disco graphy

- **Maskman** (EP)/independent, 1993
- **bionic**/Latitude Records, 1995

about when I'm writing the chord structure and the melody. I just screw around with the guitar. But when I go to write lyrics, that's when I'll think about it. The lyrics and music are two different processes most times. The songs usually have something to do with something I've seen or done or heard or thought of — rather than an event or political thing. I like that kind of music, but when I go to write, it never ends up that way.

We're serious about what we are doing and we want to keep doing it, but if doesn't work out, it's no big deal. We're not counting on it. We haven't taken out loans or anything. Anyone I've ever met from here is pretty modest and down to earth. As far as having a sense of belonging to a place, we definitely have an East Coast attitude.

MAKING MUSIC

Jason (Jay) Archibald
Guitar, vocals

Scott MacFarlane
Bass, vocals

Paul Murray
Lead vocals

Troy Shanks
Drums, piano

Mike Smith
Guitar, vocals

FANfare

Label
Latitude Records,
49 Wellington Street E., 3rd Floor,
Toronto, ON,
M5E 1C9;
(416) 361-9264 (phone);
(416) 361-9241 (fax)

Sloan

CATHERINE STOCKHAUSEN

Halifax band Sloan's so-called break-up was one of the most hotly reported stories in Canadian music in 1995. All the eulogies had one thing in common: they were premature in their presumption that Sloan was no more. After a brief hiatus, the group returned to the Canadian music scene in 1995 with their fourth album, *One Chord to Another*. Among the band's many accolades, the most dazzling was *Chart* magazine's industry insider poll that named Sloan's third release *Twice Removed* as the best Canadian album — of all time! In creating their own label, Murderecords, Sloan continues to walk the road less travelled, and they're having a good time while they are at it!

All About Making Records

[Interview with Chris Murphy]

Although I loved the Beatles as a little kid, what really blew my head off in the second grade was KISS. I took guitar lessons in third grade, but I never actually got on the guitar; I was just clapping. I basically wanted to paint my face like KISS and play guitar. I took percussion lessons in junior high, but I couldn't read music and I was eventually kicked out of that because I just wanted to play on the drum set. I can play drums and guitar and bass, but I never really learned piano, even though my mother insisted that I learn it. When I wasn't interested, she said I'd be sorry. Of course, I'm furious now.

I know that Jay was also super into KISS as a young kid. He is a rock 'n' roll historian. He has a huge record collection and was on *Switchback*, a kids' TV show, with his record collection when he was in junior high. He started working at a record store called Old Dan's when he was twelve. All he reads and watches is music; he just listens to records all day. He's the visionary of our group. Although he doesn't write the most songs, he has all the history.

Patrick came from Sackville, a little more of a hard-rocking place to come from, outside Halifax. He and I were both into heavy metal as teenagers. KISS led to Rush to Van Halen. Although Patrick is made out to be the rocker of the group, he writes the most sensitive, earnest songs of all. He is this classic dichotomy of a hard-nosed tear-jerker.

Andrew is from Dartmouth, across the bridge. He insists that his big paradox was that he carried a trombone case with a Tigers of Pangtang decal on it. Tigers is complete British metal. He taught himself to play piano. He is the most musically sophisticated, a completely brilliant musician. He's the best guitar player in the band, but he's stuck behind the drums, furious that we are all a bunch of hacks. I'm the bass player, which is supposed to be the lowest on the totem pole.

---

opening notes

Jay Ferguson
Date of birth
October 14, 1968

Place of birth
Halifax, Nova Scotia

Current residence
Halifax, Nova Scotia

Chris Murphy
Date of birth
November 7, 1968

Place of birth
Charlottetown,
Prince Edward Island

Current residence
Halifax, Nova Scotia

(more ...)

Photo, clockwise from top left:
Patrick, Chris, Andrew, Jay

opening notes

Patrick Pentland
Date of birth
September 20, 1969

Place of birth
Northern Ireland

Current residence
Halifax, Nova Scotia

Andrew Scott
Date of birth
November 15, 1967

Place of birth
Ottawa, Ontario

Current residence
Toronto, Ontario

MAKING MUSIC

Jay Ferguson
Guitar, vocals

Chris Murphy
Bass, vocals

Patrick Pentland
Guitar, vocals

Andrew Scott
Drums, vocals

If we had grown up in bigger cities, we might not have been exposed to each other. There would have been a club specifically designed for my musical tastes, and then one for each of the others. Here, there were only a couple of places that had live music. In fact, the first couple of shows that I went to, shows with both punk and heavy-metal bands, I thought that everybody would be at war with each other, but everybody got along just fine. Everybody gravitated there, even people with very disparate musical tastes. Because the place was so small, everybody was influenced by each other.

I was playing in a completely hardcore punk band, but I was also playing with Jay. I started to play with Andrew, who was a DJ at a local club here. Then Jay joined and then Patrick joined. It's musical-chairs with bands. You record some stuff, then you change members. When Sloan was discovered, the musical chairs game stopped, like, "Freeze!" Suddenly there was the band, and we were supposed to make a professional career out of the people we were with. We hadn't known Patrick for long, yet we were supposed to be in a professional career relationship with him. It was really awkward at first, and it's still awkward at times now. But I think we get along fine.

The most important thing to me is to keep the integrity of our band, the four members. We broke up at the end of 1994 because we had a lot of arguments. We could have changed members, but I was really not interested in doing that. It's the chemistry of the band that's most important. After KISS changed members in 1980, I didn't listen to them. That's where Sloan's strength is: four people willing to share the spotlight.

We are about recording. We've never been the best live band. A lot of earlier bands made records and tried to reproduce them

discography

- **Peppermint** (EP)/Murderecords, 1992
- **Smeared**/David Geffen Co., 1992
- **Twice Removed**/David Geffen Co., 1994
- **One Chord To Another**/Murderecords, 1995

on stage. Then in the late 1960s people who had great live bands — The Who, Jimi Hendrix — tried to reproduce on record the songs the way they were on stage. I think that's the difference between pop and rock. With pop music, first you formulate it, then you learn how to play it. Whereas, in rock, you're playing, then you learn to record it. We are more of a pop band. There're a lot of rock bands that still tour like maniacs and probably make a lot of money doing it. They think of their records as afterthoughts. We are definitely the opposite. We are all about making records.

We have our own record label in Canada, Murderecords. We can make the records cheaply without any interference. If anybody wants to be involved with us in business, we'll listen, but nobody can tell us what to do. That's an awesome position of power. It might mean that no one wants to be involved with us, but I think that our records are commercially viable. I also think it's about more than just the music. I think that part of it is about politics and history. We are about making history. We are totally about our community, too. We've tried to reach back and put out records that document the entire music scene here.

FAN fare

Management
Chip Sutherland,
Pier 21 Artist Management Ltd.,
5151 George Street, Suite 1701,
Halifax, NS,
B3J 1M5;
(902) 492-2100 (phone);
(902) 492-3738 (fax);
pier21@fox.nstn.ca (e-mail)

"In bigger cities, we might not have been exposed to each other."

Square and Straight

When I entered high school, everybody was into drinking and smoking and drugs. Since I was really not into that, I attached myself to this whole punk-rock movement called Straight Edge, which was all about not drinking and not smoking. It originated in Washington, DC, where the drinking age is twenty-one, and the bouncers would mark your hand with an X if you were underage. If you were Straight Edge, you put the X on your hand before you even showed up at the bar. To me it was a way to avoid peer pressure. It was, like, "I don't drink, but I'm not this uncool kid in the corner. I am the punk-rock toughest kid in the group and I'm not doing any of this." Basically I was terrified; I didn't want to drink and smoke dope. I never have, and neither has Jay. That's one of our bonds. When he and I started to play music together in 1987, it wasn't based on that, but that's been a big bond for us — that we're both completely square and straight.

Laura Smith

After a long career as a singer and songwriter, Laura Smith has suddenly come into her own. In 1996, Laura won the ECMA Female Artist of the Year and Album of the Year. Her first single release, "Shade of Your Love," has been a top ten hit across Canada, and her stunning version of the old Scottish song "My Bonny" has been as popular. She has completed five cross-Canada tours, appeared on *Rita & Friends*, participated in a live concert recording of material by the late Stan Rogers, and has enjoyed several U.S. festival and concert appearances.

Dedicated to the Song

I became a professional musician by persistence, I guess. I think being a professional means being dedicated. I started playing guitar and writing songs when I was about nineteen. I think I borrowed my first guitar. My first performance came when I was about twenty-two. I was working at a folk club as a waitress and cook in London, and finally I got up and performed. Then I started performing for friends, then at concerts and festivals in London, Ontario, and the Festival of Friends in Hamilton.

My musical influences came from listening to my brothers' record collection, Bob Dylan, Joni Mitchell, Paul Simon and Laura Nyro. Just great song writers. Joni Mitchell and Laura Nyro I think helped; somehow, listening to them, it proved to me that I had a voice, that I had things worth saying, that I could channel my emotional energy into song. That it was a workable craft. I love poetry. Being able to combine words and music is very emotionally satisfying.

In this country it would have been foolish to set being a professional songwriter as my goal because of the low esteem in which they are held. What's valued are mass success and radio hits. I didn't even consider making it my goal. My goal was to not do anything that would jeopardize my ability to write. The right way for me is not the right way for everyone. But I had limits on my coping mechanisms. I tried to play in places where music was an aside and found it very disheartening. I don't know if it was vanity, wanting to be listened to, I just knew it wasn't for me.

In my early twenties, when I started writing, I noticed a lot of people burning themselves out in bars, and on the road. I knew that I couldn't survive that. So I took any job I could and waited until people came to me. I just kept writing the songs that I write, hoping that someone would hear them and like them. And that's what happened. I was able to record a first CD with CBC Halifax.

opening notes

Date of birth
March 18, 1952

Place of birth
London, Ontario

Heritage
Irish, Scottish, Italian

Language
English

Current residence
Halifax, Nova Scotia

Instruments
Vocals, guitar

> "I believe in people and I believe in new birth."

The CBC played it nationally and then I got a call from the Festival Boreal. That was my first gig in years. To me that was worth waiting for. I didn't have a persona; there was no image to go with it. Someone just heard the songs and hired me.

My partner at the time, who was a fiddler, brought me to Cape Breton in the 1980s. I've never identified myself as an East Coast musician. There are enough great people who really exemplify the best of East Coast music in the traditional sense. I'm an East Coast musician only by virtue of living here. That's as far as it goes with me. I can't define East Coast music, except to say that it's just good.

Living here has been inspiring, though. When I leased back my first album from the CBC, I formed a company to do business under the name Cornermuse. I lived in a corner apartment with a bay window overlooking Citadel Hill, here in Halifax. I had set up the chairs and table to always be looking out — I did all of my writing there and could reach a state of amusement just by sitting in my favourite chair — the familiar posture and view signaled to my brain that self-hypnosis could begin and creativity would not be blocked. I made "My Bonny," "Gypsy Dream," "Clean Up Your Own Backyard," "So Close to My Knees" and "Duine Air Call" sitting in that window (all on *B'tween the Earth and My Soul*).

I feel very much for the people here who are losing their traditional ways of earning a living off the sea. I fear a real brain drain of the young, the vital ones who have ideas and who keep Nova Scotia from turning into Plymouth Rock-type towns where everything is historic and there is no present — those little towns that tourism dollars have propped up. I'm mindful of things that seem to be disappearing. I think it is important to keep listening, stay open, not judge anyone. I do believe in people and I believe in new birth.

discography

- **Laura Smith**/CBC Maritimes, 1989
- **B'tween the Earth and My Soul**/Cornermuse Recordings, 1994

I think it's important for young people to take the time after they have learned everything about the subject they have chosen and have graduated to look around and remember where they came from and what they value most about their lives. They should at least try to find one thing they value the most. Then, with as much grace and humour and talent as they can muster, they should make sure they work to preserve it.

> **FAN fare**
>
> **Management**
> Jones & Co.,
> 1819 Granville Street, 4th Floor,
> Halifax, NS,
> B3J 3R1;
> (902) 429-9005 (phone);
> (902) 429-9071 (fax)

Dry Bones

There was a bone player, named Wild Archie MacLellan, who was very famous around Sydney. I had learned to play the Irish drum, the bodhran, and I was fascinated by these ribs, beef ribs, that he had made his bones with. I wanted to learn to play and have a set of my own. He told me to go to the butcher and ask for two rib bones. He even told me which ribs. I had arranged to pick him up at the seniors' home where he lived and bring him home for supper. By then I'd have the ribs and he'd teach me how to play them.

Well, I went to the butcher and made my request. He said that I would have to come back the next day. The next day he had the entire side of a cow for me. One whole side of the rib cage, a bloody raw rib cage.

I took the rib cage home and I just stared at it, close to tears, because it was time to pick up Wild Archie and I was supposed to have my bones ready. I took a saw and I cut off the two ribs I thought I was supposed to use and put them in the oven on low. Then I picked Wild Archie from the seniors' home. By the time I got back I had two really hard, crispy bones in the oven. I showed Wild Archie the rib cage, and though he didn't say anything, we knew I wasn't going to learn to play the bones on my set. It was a pretty humiliating event. I never did learn how to play the bones.

Sons of Membertou

Back row, left to right: Dawn Isadore, Sharon Bernard, Darrell Bernard, George Christmas, Puddy Christmas
Beside and behind drum, left to right: Lonnie Jones, Patrick Christmas, Graham Marshall, Aussi Christmas
Front, left to right: John K. McEwan, Craig Hodder

The gathering, or powwow, is a traditional celebration that brings people together at certain times of the year to socialize, to celebrate life, to rejuvenate the spirit and to dance and pray with the ancestors. Sons of Membertou is a musical reflection of the spirit of the powwow. The group started in 1992 with four members doing traditional songs and chants in their First Nation community of Membertou. As interest developed, the group grew and has performed at countless powwows, gatherings and festivals. Their first album, *Wapna'kik, "The People of the Dawn,"* combines the traditional sound of the Native drums with the contemporary sounds of some of Cape Breton's finest musicians.

NATALIE MCEWAN

Taking Pride in Who We Are

[Interview with Darrell Bernard, Drum Keeper]

Our name comes from Membertou the person, not from the community. He was a very important chief in Mi'kmaq history. He died in 1616, when he was 110 years old. He opened up the communication with Europe.

My wife and I were given the responsibility of keeping the drum by the elders. We were asked to start a young people's group to divert some of the young people who are poor from the temptations of living in Sydney and everything that is out there. These temptations are more common in the Native communities, but they are also part of being unemployed and not having a whole lot going on. I was given the drum by the Council of Elders in Membertou in November 1992. I approached Graham Marshall, and a couple of other guys who aren't with us any more. Graham was pretty young, thirteen at the time, but he already knew a lot of songs and had a lot to offer. He leads quite a few of our songs now.

It's all men who sit and drum at the big drums. Women use hand drums or shakers. That's the way we were taught, but it's changing too. There are mixed groups out there where women also sit at the drum. The woman is the centre of the home, of the family, the teacher of the family. The man is just a provider. We are not equal. The woman is on a higher spiritual plane. She is more important in the family. She's in charge of the family, and she is usually the better-looking out of the two!

I had quite a bit of learning to do about our traditions. The elders themselves were probably the ones who did most of the teaching.

---

opening notes

Darrell Bernard

Date of birth
April 6, 1960

Place of birth
Membertou, Cape Breton (NS)

Heritage
Mi'kmaq

Languages
English, Mi'kmaq

Current residence
Membertou, Cape Breton (NS)

MAKING MUSIC

Group members: Darell Bernard, Sharon Bernard, Aussi Christmas, George Christmas, Clifford Coppage, Craig Hodder, Dawn Isadore, J.R. Isadore, Lonnie Jones, John K. McEwan, B.J. Marshall, Graham Marshall, Shane Paul
Drums, vocals

> "Having respect for each other is really, really important."

We also had a lot of assistance from other Aboriginal people involved in the music industry, not just the traditional music scene. Native people across Canada have a whole different circle. We call it the Powwow Trail. We get together in just about every Native community — not just our Mi'kmaq people, but Aboriginal people from around North America. There are many different powwows during the summer. Drum groups get together and perform. It's a lot of fun. It's a good social, spiritual gathering. We also have a traditional spirtual gathering called a *Mawawiowi*.

The powwow has a spiritual aspect, too. Ceremonies take place and we use the sweat lodge. Certain people have different roles that they have earned and worked for. To be a drummer in a drum group is a way of life. We have certain things that we can do and certain things that we don't participate in. Most drummers stay completely away from alcohol and drugs, and any that don't must stay away from the drum for a certain amount of time. It's a spiritual lifestyle in a way.

People in general are looking toward Aboriginal teachings and traditional teachings because they make a lot more sense now that preserving the environment is so important. Things that our people talked about so long ago, things that seemed impossible at the time, like the fish disappearing and the sky opening up and the sun burning everybody, aren't impossible any more. People are opening their eyes and looking at other teachings. We don't have all the answers, but there are some things that we want to share. Having respect for each other is really, really important. I know that all cultures teach this.

Returning to our roots has everything to do with finding ourselves. We have brought back our old songs and our traditional regalia. A lot of the ceremonial stuff that was hidden away for so many years is now more acceptable. To be unique is okay nowadays.

discography

- *Wapna'kik*, **The People of the Dawn**/independent, 1995

It's become important to let people know that we are here and that we have some ancient things that we would like to share. Some of the songs that we do are really, really old songs. Some of them are so old that they don't even translate any more, not into contemporary Mi'kmaq, let alone into English.

Some of the music we do is new. We're having a great time doing it. We have the opportunity to play in a lot of places. Among others, we played three sets at the G-7 Summit; we played for the world leaders, to the wives of the world leaders.

I think our elders are proud of what we are doing. I know we are. When we perform here in our community, we have our guys sitting around the drum, but we also have twenty kids sitting around the drum and doing songs in Mi'kmaq. They are able to do this thing that is completely unique to them. It's theirs. Our people have been going out into the society for so long and flipping to page four in their Social Studies books and seeing half a page on Mi'kmaqs. If you looked in the history books twenty years ago, you'd see very little about the Mi'kmaq people and our relationships with the English or the French or anybody. We accepted that we were disappearing at that time, but now we say, "We are here. It's good we survived and we are going to continue." We take great pride in who we are.

FAN fare

Management
Sons of Membertou,
29 Veteran's Avenue,
Membertou, NS,
B1S 3K8;
(902) 539-5960 (phone);
(902) 539-2868 (fax);
kukes@atcon.com (e-mail)

Smoke

We played at the Savoy Theatre in Glace Bay, Cape Breton. We were burning sweetgrass in the dressing room just before the show because every time we drum we burn sweetgrass and do a little offering. One of the guys lit the sweetgrass. It was good sweetgrass and it was smoking good. He said, "The spirits are with us tonight." The second he got that out of his mouth, the fire alarm went off and we had to evacuate the building. It was a smoking performance.

Kim Stockwood

In 1990 Kim Stockwood performed a couple of songs at a folk night at her local pub in St. John's, Newfoundland. Next thing she knew, she was singing on weekends. As her reputation grew, she decided to move to Toronto. In 1993 Kim headed down the road for the big city with a suitcase and guitar, seeking fame and fortune. Within two months, she had a publishing deal with EMI Music Publishing, which led to a recording deal with EMI Music Canada. Her debut release, *Bonavista,* has yielded her a hit single "Jerk." Kim's smarts and sense of humour are balanced by strong songwriting talents and great vocal delivery. It has only just begun for this gutsy and talented Newfoundlander.

Staying True to Myself

I'm from Newfoundland. I live it, breathe it, love it. Anyone who thinks that, because I pay rent in Toronto, I'm not from Newfoundland — well, I am! I wear it on my face, on my sleeve, in my heart — as do most Newfoundlanders. I am proud to be from where I'm from. I think it's given me an advantage, an insight into things that some people don't have. We make our living off the water, or at least we did. That adds a different perspective on things.

We grew up outside St. John's, in Mount Pearl. My mother and grandmother grew up in Bonavista, the name of my record. My father is from a little place called Gull Island, which is around Northern Bay Sands and Lower Island Cove. It's the same area Sean McCann from Great Big Sea is from. Sean and I are fourth cousins or something, so I guess we'll never get married.

There wasn't a lot of music in my family, although my father played the accordion, and my grandmother played the church organ. On my dad's side, there was lots of humour. Lots of playing the spoons. I grew up with the spoons. I bought a set of homemade spoons in Gander when I was playing there. They're a bit of a cheater set, a handle with two spoons stuck together. They are very cool.

My father is an amazing accordion player. I keep teasing him about coming to Toronto to do a show with me, but he hasn't yet. I bought an accordion a while ago, but I haven't had time to learn it. I want to play it as a tribute to my father. Obviously I'm not going to play it like he does, because he has a button accordion. Mine is a keyboard one, because I took classical piano for ten years. I was a streetwise kind of piano player. I always got to perform last in the recital. I wasn't that good, but I had the feel. I had the passion for it. I might not have had the technical know-how, but I had the emotion.

When I was growing up, I listened to my father's music, everything from Waylon Jennings to Al Martino. Dad had very eclectic

opening notes

Date of birth
November 11, 1965; Scorpio

Place of birth
St. John's, Newfoundland

Heritage
English (Devon)

Current residence
Toronto, Ontario

Instruments
Guitar, piano, accordion, vocals

> "I am the same kind of crazy Newf wherever I go."

tastes. I remember listening to the traditional stuff, but I don't know what it was. I just remember the fireplace going on Saturday nights in the winter when I was seven or eight years old. We would listen to Roy Payne, Dick Nolan and all this old kind of stuff, and then we would listen to Al Martino and the Tijuana Brass and the Ventures. When I came into my teens, god forbid, I liked Shawn Cassidy and Leif Garrett. I had J. Geils on 8-track.

I've been a lot of places in the past couple of years, and basically what it all comes down to is, do you know yourself well enough to take your little person and put yourself anywhere else in the world and be the same person. I think, luckily for me, I am the same crazy kind of Newf wherever I go. I feel proud of that because it's a test of my character. It took me a long time to build myself. It's like building a friggin' house. You build yourself as you grow and get older. You learn about yourself. It takes you a long time to know what you like about yourself. When you do, you hang onto that stuff. One of my boyfriends told me he didn't like the fact that I used to jump up on piano stools and sing. He thought I was too weird or something. Well that's what got me my EMI deal. That's who I am and I'm going to do it.

I strive to be a good person. That's my goal in life. When I die, I want people to remember that about me. I don't want them to remember that I was a rock star or that I did this or that. I want them to say Kim was a really good person. I am constantly trying to make my parents proud of me. I'm sure that they are proud, but the rock 'n' roll stuff isn't what makes them proud. They don't give a shit about that — which is great, because they constantly bring me back down to earth.

It's a powerful feeling to know that you can affect people's lives by something that you do. For me it just happens to be singing and writing. It could have been something else, and, for a lot of times,

discography

- **Bonavista**/EMI Music Canada, 1995
- **Bonavista** (revised)/EMI Music Canada, 1996

it was. I've always done things that were in the communication field. I co-hosted a morning show in Newfoundland and I was a copywriter for an ad agency and I was a PR person for a communications firm. I've always done things that used my personality, I always will. I want to do some acting someday. I don't know if I could do it, but I'd love to try. And dance too. I'd do my little Mikey Jackson moves — with a rock 'n' roll accordion.

My advice is to believe in what you do. Be able to accept rejection. Know what you can and cannot change. You have to know what you're good at and what you're not good at, but it takes a long time and you have to have patience with it. Believe in what you do. It's hard sometimes. For me the song "Jerk" is proof that you can never give up. Right before that song was written, I seriously thought about quitting and going back to Newfoundland because I missed it so much and my career was not where I wanted it to be. Out of the blue, with that song, my life completely changed in a matter of four months. You never know what's going to happen.

FANfare

Management
The Bob Roper Co.,
P.O. Box 43147,
325 Central Parkway West,
Mississauga, ON,
L5E 3X0;
(905) 848-8868 (phone);
(905) 848-1781 (fax)

Promotions
EMI Music Canada, Halifax Sales and Promotion Office,
18 Savona Court,
Dartmouth, NS,
B2W 4R1;
(902) 434-9520 (phone/fax)

Crying for Elvis

When I was about eleven, I saw a movie with this guy Elvis in it. It was my awakening. Up until then, truthfully, I didn't know who he was. Elvis wasn't getting played on my radio, because I was listening to Meatloaf and stuff on the top ten. I knew nothing about him until I saw this movie and I went wow!! He was young and cool and I started thinking, "Man, I want to marry this guy." I thought he was as young as he was on the movie. The next day I told Mom, I'm going to meet Elvis Presley. I'm going to Graceland, and I'm going to meet him. I was eleven years old.

A year later, in 1977, he died. I thought that was the end of my life, because I was never going to get to meet Elvis, and I was never going to get to go to Graceland. I was shattered. I sat home that night. It was a really hot night. I turned on the radio. All night, they played Elvis. I made a Kraft sausage pizza and ate almost the entire thing. Sat on the floor listening to Elvis and cried and cried and cried.

I was so sick after that I didn't give a shit that Elvis died. I just wanted my stomach to get better.

Suroît

"Suroît" means "southwest wind," a name chosen by the band to show they are "Maritimers right to the bone."

It is not easy to describe the music played by Suroît, the Madgalen Islands' hottest musical export. The five members come from varied musical backgrounds and play so many instruments there seems to be little room to move when they take to the stage. But move they do, and so does the audience. Their sound was once described as "white soul music." And every member will tell you that they put their soul into every gig. Soul and a genuine love of the music have kept them touring and playing since the late 1970s. They have had nine concert trips to France, several outings across Canada, and a deal with one of Quebec's top record companies.

In the Middle of All Kinds of Music

[Interview with Alcide Painchaud and Kenneth Saulnier]

Alcide: We're right in the middle of all kinds of music. We grew up in a mix of Quebec and Maritime culture. Our music has Celtic influences, and the words of our songs have a French influence. Since we're Acadian, our songs belong to the Acadian culture in the Maritimes. And we are also influenced by Louisiana culture.

Kenneth: All the people in the group come from the Magdalen Islands except me, but I feel very akin to the Islands. There is the same musical mentality there as where I grew up. I was brought up down home in St. Mary's Bay, Nova Scotia, which is known as the French Shore, between Digby and Yarmouth. I'm from the village of Saulnierville Station. I started playing music at an early age. The whole family would play together. There were a lot of musicians and a lot of different clubs and groups. Even before I was old enough to go into a legion hall, I was in a band playing with these older people. From there I went to Moncton, New Brunswick, to pursue my studies. At that time I started professionally on the road. Up till then I had just played music in English. Being close to the United States, most of the people down home were influenced by the Americans, all the bluegrass, country and Maritime fiddling.

Alcide: Everyone on my father's side of the family sang. My aunt and a cousin were opera singers. I have a couple of aunts who were great ragtime players. On that side we had singing parties all the time. They started around ten o'clock in the evening and would last till morning. On my mother's side they were all musicians: piano and accordion and organ players. I've been a professional on the

---

opening notes

Alcide Painchaud
Date of birth
October 29, 1948

Place of birth
Magdalen Islands, Quebec

Current residence
Quebec City, Quebec

Kenneth Saulnier
Date of birth
April 7, 1956

Place of birth
Halifax, Nova Scotia

Current residence
Quebec City, Quebec

Photo, clockwise from top:
Henri-Paul, Réal, Alcide, Félix, Kenneth

MAKING MUSIC

Henri-Paul Bénard
Vocals, acoustic guitar, mandolin, bones, spoons, harmonica, accordion, washboard

Félix Leblanc
Vocals, violin, tap

Réal Longuépée
Vocals, acoustic & electric bass

Alcide Painchaud
Accordion, vocals, piano, synthesizer

Kenneth Saulnier
Banjo, acoustic & electric guitar, dobro, mandolin, violin, vocals

road for a long time. I started to play in dance halls when I was only thirteen years old. By the late 1970s I got back to traditional music. That is when I got up this group.

Kenneth: When I started playing in Moncton, we couldn't play a whole night in French. It wasn't well accepted. Once Quebec rock groups like Harmonium and Beaux Domage became popular, it really got me rolling to do French music. It did not take long for the group I was with, called 1755, to stop doing English songs. We were into our Acadian identity. This pride in identity that Quebec initiated, created a movement in the Maritimes; people realized that they had a French identity and they should be proud of it. All of a sudden it spread like wildfire everywhere. It just woke up the people. That was from 1975 to 1979.

Alcide: At the very beginning we were on the road a lot. We were in the States for over two years. We played 125 times with the first incarnation of Suroît. Then, by the 1980s, when the discotèques took over, it was hard to survive with a live group. Everybody did something on the side. In 1992, we got back together and re-formed the group that exists now.

By the late 1980s people got sick of hearing canned music. They wanted to get back to live music. Every region in every country started to pick up their own thing and put some very lively renewal into their old traditional stuff. Every international festival we do, we meet people from Africa, from the Indian Ocean, from Europe and from here in Canada and the States. Everyone's got their own "home" material and they are putting it on the air now. That's the worldbeat: everybody being together and mixing the sound of many cultures.

Kenneth: When I left the Maritimes, I thought we had to go to Quebec because that is where the big population is. When I got to

discography

- **Suroît**/Suroît/G.S.I., 1989
- **Ressac**/Suroît/G.S.I., 1993

Quebec I found it wasn't exactly a piece of cake there. It was tough. You had to push through that big scene in Montreal where certain people control the radio waves. If you don't fit into their kind of music, you don't get played. So we are still up against that, but we are getting to the people just the same. The smaller radio stations are playing our music. It is just a matter of sticking together. Those who stick together the longest will finally succeed!

I'm glad this Maritime phenomenon is happening. We live in Quebec City because our production is in Montreal, and we are in the French market. But we are still Maritimers right to the bone.

You have to be ready to accept a lot of things because this is not an ordinary job. Although you have a lot of free time, it is never the same. You visit different countries and different cultures, travelling, doing what you love the most. The work is not the music; the work is travelling, living out of suitcases, eating restaurant food all the time, not sleeping much. Since the road can be tiring, you have to manage it well and not abuse your body and soul.

Alcide: We do the thing that we love. It is for us.

> **FAN fare**
>
> Management
> Suroît,
> 2460 Pierre Boucher #2,
> Quebec City, PQ,
> G1J 3X7;
> (418) 523-4589 (phone);
> (418) 527-8255 (fax)

"World beat: everybody being together and mixing the sound of many cultures."

Up, Up, and Away

We were playing at a balloon festival in Lewiston, Maine. It was beautiful, playing music and watching all the balloons go up one at a time, right in front of our eyes. We were singing, but we were looking up in the air. All of a sudden three balloons started inflating at the same time, right behind the soundboard. They got bigger and bigger, until the soundman felt something at his back. Finally we had to stop playing because one balloon was on top of the soundboard and we were worried that our soundman was going to take off with the balloon. The crowd had to hold up the balloon so it wouldn't crush the soundboard. It was hilarious.

Duncan Wells

CAROL KENNEDY

Although Duncan Wells is known primarily as a children's entertainer, he is also a songwriter, playwright and actor for both children and adults. In addition to his children's group, Duncan and the Apple in a Tree Band, he also plays in an adult band, the Sowbelly Trio. Duncan has worked hard at educating music-industry people to the importance of children's music as a legitimate musical form. He was awarded 1996 ECMA's Children Entertainer of the Year. His songs for children combine simple melodies with clever lyrics, and range from gentle ballads to the educational message of "Sally the Magnificent Cow." His adult songs have been performed by the Rankin Family, Rita MacNeil and Patricia Conroy.

Contributing Something Lasting

My first paying gig came on my summer vacation between Grades Four and Five. I was thirteen when Kevin Cameron and a few other kids from the neighbourhood formed Kevin and the Dinkys. We played stuff like the Beatles, Paul Revere and the Raiders and whoever else was cool back then. I remember how excited we were the day we found out that Kevin had got us booked to play at Holy Redeemer gym in Whitney Pier. That first gig proved so successful that we were booked to play every Friday evening for the rest of the school year.

I was writing a lot back then, but most of it was either weird anti-everything songs or poems about girls. When I graduated from high school, I applied for work on a ship. Nine days later I was a sailor in Sarnia, Ontario, working for the Texaco Oil Company. Sailing brought a certain maturity to my writing. I began to focus more on people, faraway places and the sea. It was the sheer power and mystery of the sea and that strange feeling I got when I could look in every direction and see nothing but water and sky that really had a hold on me.

For four years in the early 1980s, four of my one-act and one of my full-length plays were brought to life for local audiences. At about that time I teamed up with another Cape Breton songwriter, Ken Chisholm, to write and produce affordable musical theatre for children, but home video was so popular that even a two-dollar admission wasn't enough to get parents to bring their children to our shows. The company folded within two years and I began a one-person production company called the Talent Project, which produced original songs and skits for children.

During all of this I was still writing for adults, playing at local bars and at parties for friends. One of those friends, Bette MacDonald, had just joined the cast of *Cape Breton Summertime Revue*, the annual musical event of the year on Cape Breton Island. Bette

---

opening notes

Date of birth
October 1, 1953; Libra

Place of birth
Sydney, Cape Breton (NS)

Heritage
Canadian

Language
English

Current residence
Sydney, Cape Breton (NS)

Instruments
Guitar, vocals

> "Performing for children makes me feel young and silly and happy."

suggested the revue give me a call. That summer I heard, for the first time, two of my songs being performed by someone else. For the next nine years the *Cape Breton Summertime Revue* performed and recorded at least one of my songs every year.

Sadly, it was not the children's music that brought me to the attention of the East Coast music industry. Children's music on the East Coast is not considered by the music business to be as valuable as other musical art forms. Songs for adults is where it's at, and for me it was the *Cape Breton Summertime Revue* that brought me credibility as an artist.

In 1990, I renewed an old musical acquaintance with David Burke, and we began what was to become Duncan and the Apple in a Tree Band. The purpose was to create a band dedicated to the performance of original songs and stories for children. Together with ex-rock 'n' rollers Carl Calder on drums and Bobby Keel on bass guitar, that's exactly what we did. We began playing schools, community halls and summer festivals. Six years later we have a huge following of children, parents and educators. The focus of the band remains the same today as it was in 1990.

David and I continue to work on new projects. We have written and performed two CBC radio specials for children. We are also working toward the production of specialty recordings for children. One is a Halloween story, the other a children's musical entitled "Kathleen and the Fiddling Cat."

I continue to write songs and scripts for both adults and children. It is, however, from the writing and performing for children that I receive the most satisfaction. I suppose it's because it makes me feel young and silly and happy. I feel that I am contributing something special to the world, something durable, lasting and timeless. I would like to think, if the planet survives its stupidity,

discography

- **Ladder to the Sky**/independent, 1993
- **T. L. C.**/Beak Music, 1994
- **Duncan Back to Back**/independent, 1995

that 100 years from now a mother will be rocking her baby in her arms somewhere singing:

> *Tell me that you love me, darling / give me all your kisses / and a flower for my hair / when the petals fall / we'll be parting / but I will always love you / daisy dear*

My hope is someday to see one of my adult songs go to number one so I can support my career as a children's entertainer.

FANfare

Management
Duncan Wells,
291 Champlain Avenue,
Sydney, NS,
B1P 6P9;
(902) 562-8884 (phone)

Playing for the Bigshots

Back in the 1970s, I received a call informing me that some very important people from the CBC were coming to Sydney and that the local station wanted to showcase the area's best talent. I couldn't believe my good fortune. I went through all the songs I had written. The love songs were silly, and the anti-everything songs were a bit too heavy. After a lot of thought, I decided to open my three-song set with "How Can I Not Miss a Girl Your Size?" which was a love song from a husband to his late overweight wife. It was the funniest thing I had ever written and I figured it would really warm up the crowd.

I was nervous when I arrived at the College Pub to perform. I remember all the expensive suits and glittering jewellery. I remember, also, thinking that this was going to be my big break. After the show was over, I'd be asked to sign an exclusive CBC contract and would never have to worry about anything ever again. I got up on the stage, adjusted my microphone and went right into it:

"How can I not miss a girl your size / how can I forget the flab / that rippled off your thighs / you left me with a grocery bill / and an empty fridge besides / how can I not miss / the way you did the twist / how can I not miss a girl your size?"

By the time I got to the chorus, Sons of Skye, another one of the acts, were falling out of their seats with laughter. I soon realized, however, that it wasn't my song that was so funny. By the time I got to the second chorus, I noticed how large all of the wives of the CBC bigshots were and how unhappy they all looked. Of course, the Sons of Skye didn't help much. They laughed hysterically through the entire song, and even when they took the stage they were still trying to wipe the smirks off their faces.

Lee Fleming

Music has always been my first passion. I grew up in a musical family and received voice training from an early age from my mother, a talented pianist with a professionally trained voice. Since my early teens, I've been playing music and writing songs. A grounding in reggae and blues came from living in the West Indies in my early twenties; playing street music taught me musical spontaneity; and my current studies in classical guitar and voice have given me the gift of discipline and humility. I am following my dream of recording a CD of original songs and I'll continue to edit books to feed my social, political and intellectual soul. I am kept grounded by my partner Heidi and her three great kids.

closing notes

Date of birth
October 13, 1957

Place of birth
Toronto, Ontario

Heritage
Hotblooded Celtic & conservative Anglo-Saxon

Languages
English, French

Current residence
Charlottetown, Prince Edward Island

Instruments
Vocals, classical & acoustic guitar, blues harp, percussion

Books
Feminist bookstore co-owner, 1982-87; *By Word of Mouth*, 1988; *Tide Lines*, 1991; *To Sappho, My Sister*, 1995; *Hot Licks*, 1996 (all with gynergy books)

JACK LECLAIR